The Motion Picture
and the
Teaching of English

The Motion Picture and the Teaching of English

MARION C. SHERIDAN DIRECTOR
HAROLD H. OWEN, JR. CHIEF WRITER
KEN MACRORIE ASSOCIATE WRITER
FRED MARCUS ASSOCIATE WRITER

PREPARED UNDER A GRANT TO THE NATIONAL COUNCIL
OF TEACHERS OF ENGLISH FROM TEACHING FILM CUS-
TODIANS, INC.

APPLETON-CENTURY-CROFTS
EDUCATIONAL DIVISION
NEW YORK **MEREDITH CORPORATION**

PRINTED IN THE UNITED STATES OF AMERICA
390–80420–7

NCTE Committee on Publications

Foreword

This book is designed to help a viewer look at motion pictures perceptively. It might well have been titled *How Does a Motion Picture Mean?* It seeks to reveal *how,* which is in many ways different from the way a book or a play communicates. In addition to this emphasis on understanding the unique characteristics of film as an art form, the book discusses the role of motion pictures in the English program.

In its ability to compress and play with time, film is like the novel. Yet it is superior in its ability to flash back, to coalesce experiences occurring in different times, and to move ahead and transcend time. It is unique in its ability to render the world of the dream and the subconscious. In many respects it is like poetry, in that it proceeds by metaphor and analogy. As the poet and his reader "see feelingly," through the medium of words, so the film maker and the viewer see feelingly through the medium of pictures, with an empathy just as great as, and often greater than, that which the reader feels.

Film has a special quality which no one has yet satisfactorily named. It is something like immediacy or instantaneousness, an astonishing and total impact on the senses. This immediacy may be disarming: the capacity of film for examining life, through the concrete image, is extraordinary; the sense of reality inherent in the form is overwhelming. The motion picture, a result of twentieth-century technology, like other mass media relying on a mass audience for its economic survival, is subject to limitation, stereotype, and dilution. But when a well-made film is produced, it has a power not yet equaled by that of any other medium to capture and satisfy the mass audience.

The bulk of those attending films are in their teens and

twenties. The reasons are complex. The demands of family life, economic factors, and the presence of television are partly responsible. So are the many mediocre films. Their mediocrity is due as much to the failure of critics and teachers to develop critical audiences as it is to an underestimation on the part of the motion picture industry about the taste and demands of the public. Granted that a kind of Gresham's law operates where mass culture is concerned, so that the easy and spurious tend to displace the difficult and true; such a fact does not prevent the critic from trying to discriminate between the two, nor the English teacher from facing the responsibility of defining the excellent.

Because this book makes its points through numerous examples from actual films, the reader should not infer that the authors are praising the complete film from which any one example is taken or recommending the film for students. Nor is it necessary for the reader to assume that he must see all the films cited in order to understand the point being made. This is a book about how to look at film, not a listing of "great" or "educational" films.

There are many reasons why we have considered the role of the moving picture in the teaching of English. First, the film has an unparalleled power to transmit information and inferences. Second, it may illuminate and augment the study of literature. Third, it has form, structure, theme, irony, metaphor, and symbol—aspects of any work of art, and hence subject to examination and isolation. And finally, it is concerned with ethics, values, and truth—which may be embodied or distorted in films as in any other medium.

The authors of this book believe that if the teacher already skilled in literary analysis is aware of how a film communicates, he will be able on his own to devise exercises and demonstrations which will acquaint others with the unique process of film. Therefore the book concentrates on the essential differences between film and other media and provides suggestions for the teacher in the classroom only incidentally, or by implication.

This book has been made possible through a grant from Teaching Film Custodians, Incorporated, a nonprofit corporation (established in 1938) which seeks to enrich education by making available film material from productions of theatrical motion picture producing companies. For some years a committee from the National Council of Teachers of English has worked closely with TFC in preparing excerpts from feature-length pictures, as well as guides to accompany them. The work of preparing these excerpts and the guides led to a consideration of the wisdom and the possibility of producing a book for classroom teachers. TFC awarded a grant to the National Council of Teachers of English in order to develop this book.

The writers are indebted to a number of people for their sponsorship and counsel: to Stanley McIntosh, Executive Director, Teaching Film Custodians, as well as to the Board of Directors of that organization; to James R. Squire, Executive Secretary of the National Council of Teachers of English; and to the National Advisory Committee, whose disinterested and experienced recommendations have been of immeasurable help. This committee includes the following:

Robert B. Carruthers, Associate Supervisor of English, State Department of Education, Albany, New York

Mrs. Esmer K. Clark, Director of Secondary Curriculum, Berkeley Schools, Berkeley, California

Richard Corbin, Chairman of the English Department, Hunter College High School, New York City; First Vice President (1964), National Council of Teachers of English

Hardy R. Finch, Supervisor of English, Public Schools, Greenwich, Connecticut

Patrick D. Hazard, Chairman of the English Department, Beaver College, Glenside, Pennsylvania

Joseph Mersand, Chairman of the English Department, Jamaica High School, Jamaica, New York; Editor, *Studies in the Mass Media*

Robert C. O'Hara, Assistant Professor of English, College of Liberal Arts, University of South Florida, Tampa, Florida

Walter J. Ong, S.J., Professor of English, St. Louis University, St. Louis, Missouri

Ethel C. Tincher, Supervisor of Language Education Department and Director of Television Teaching Program, Public Schools, Detroit, Michigan

Samuel D. Wehr, Professor of Education, Temple University, Philadelphia, Pennsylvania.

Helen Olson, Director of English, Public Schools, and Edna Sterling, formerly Director of English, Public Schools, Seattle, Washington, considered the manuscript in relation to the classroom.

Thanks are due to a number of people who offered ideas and material that proved invaluable. Alex E. Alden, Society of Motion Picture and Television Engineers, made helpful suggestions increasing understanding of new techniques. Robert Dye, Western Michigan University, contributed many insights into *Citizen Kane*; Robert C. O'Hara enlarged concepts of the stereotype; Patrick D. Hazard reminded us constantly of the historical framework without which contemporary affairs are incomprehensible; and the Reverend Walter J. Ong, S.J., gave advice and encouragement from a humanistic viewpoint.

The Production Team are indebted to Paul V. Beckley, motion picture critic; the Reverend John M. Culkin, S.J., studying at Harvard University, 1962-1964; and Norman N. Holland, Associate Professor of English, Department of Humanities, Massachusetts Institute of Technology, for critical reading of the manuscript and discerning, detailed comments. Other consultant readers who offered helpful suggestions were

Father C. B. McNamee, S.J., Chairman, English Department, Saint Louis University; John P. Noonan, Director of Freshman English, Kansas State University; Elizabeth S. Wright, Assistant Superintendent, Bucks County Public Schools, Pennsylvania; and Robert F. Hogan, Associate Executive Secretary, NCTE.

The Production Team immediately responsible for the preparation of this book include the following:

Project Director: Marion C. Sheridan, Consultant in English, 1057 Whitney Avenue, Hamden, Connecticut; Chairman, National Council of Teachers of English Committee to Cooperate with Teaching Film Custodians, Inc.; former President, National Council of Teachers of English

Chief Writer: Harold H. Owen, Jr., Phillips Academy, Andover, Massachusetts

Associate Writer: Ken Macrorie, Associate Professor of English, Western Michigan University, Kalamazoo, Michigan; Editor, *College Composition and Communication*

Associate Writer: Fred H. Marcus, Professor of English, Los Angeles State College, Los Angeles, California

Liaison with Teaching Film Custodians, Inc.: John E. Braslin, Director of Curriculum Materials, Teaching Film Custodians, Inc.

Liaison with the National Council of Teachers of English: Robert A. Bennett, Specialist in Language Arts, City Schools, San Diego, California; Chairman, Secondary Section, National Council of Teachers of English (1960-1962).

Acknowledgments

The authors and publishers are grateful to the following people for permission to use in this book illustrative excerpts from other publications and photographs from films:

William D. Baker for permission to reprint in Appendix B his article, "Film as Sharpener of Perception," from the February 1964 issue of *College Composition and Communication*.

Beta Phi Mu for permission to reprint excerpts from Frances H. Flaherty, *The Odyssey of a Film-Maker; Robert Flaherty's Story* (Urbana, Ill.: Beta Phi Mu, 1960). Used by permission of Beta Phi Mu and Frances H. Flaherty.

Dorothy Chamberlain for permission to reprint excerpts from Otis Ferguson's review of *The Grapes of Wrath* in *The New Republic* for February 12, 1940.

Columbia Pictures Corporation for permission to reprint the photo from *On the Waterfront* on page 66. Used by courtesy of Columbia Pictures.

Esquire Magazine for permission to reprint excerpts from columns by Dwight Macdonald in the May 1962 and January 1963 issues, © 1962 by Esquire, Inc., and reprinted by permission of *Esquire* Magazine.

Janus Films for permission to reprint the photo from *L'Avventura* on page 6.

Metro-Goldwyn-Mayer, Inc., for permission to reprint the series of eight photos from *The Search* on pages 24-25. Copyright Loew's International Corporation, 1948.

The New Republic for permission to reprint excerpts from two articles by Stanley Kauffman: "Exercises in Pathos and Politics," June 4, 1962, and "An Artist for an Age," Feb-

ruary 26, 1962. Reprinted from *The New Republic,* ©
Harrison-Blaine, Inc.

The New Yorker for permission to reprint excerpts from an
article by Brendan Gill: "The Current Cinema—Out of the
Dark," June 2, 1962. Used by permission of *The New
Yorker* and Brendan Gill.

RKO Radio Pictures, a division of RKO General, Inc., for
permission to reprint the photo from *Citizen Kane* on page
21.

Sight and Sound for permission to reprint in Appendix A an
excerpt from Norman Fruchter's "two 2 hours a week" in
its Autumn 1962 issue.

Simon and Schuster, Inc., for permission to reprint excerpts
from Leonard Bernstein, *The Joy of Music* (New York:
Simon and Schuster, 1959).

Time Magazine for permission to reprint an excerpt from "A
Religion of Film" in the September 20, 1963, issue of *Time.*
Courtesy *Time;* © Time Inc. 1963.

United Artists Corporation for permission to reprint photos
from *The Miracle Worker* on page 59, © MCMLXII by
Playfilm Productions, Inc.; from *West Side Story* on page
69, © Copyright MCMLXI by Beta Productions; from
Hamlet on pages 44 and 76, Courtesy the Rank Organization; and *Henry V* on pages 35, 36, and 77, Courtesy the
Rank Organization. All rights reserved.

Contents

Contents

The Motion Picture
and the
Teaching of English

CHAPTER ONE

Space, Time, and Image

An American health expert once showed a film on combating malaria to a group who had never before seen a film. After seeing an enormous close-up of a mosquito, one viewer complained, "This film is of no use to us. We don't have mosquitoes that large."

This story indicates the utter willingness of the observer to assume the reality of film. In a novel, words must conjure up the pictures; they are the medium. In film, pictures are the medium. Those of us nurtured in a print-bound world are at home with a story told in words. We can follow it, read its meanings on several levels, and look at it critically as a work of art. We are not so familiar with the language of film, and in our lack of awareness of film techniques we may not read it on its various levels or grasp the meanings implanted by the film's director.

If we are to get as much of what is in a film as we do of what is in a play by Shakespeare, we shall have to learn how a film director achieves his work of art as we once learned how Shakespeare achieved his.

A VISUAL MEDIUM

Film is primarily a visual medium, not a verbal one. Its vocabulary and grammar are composed of individual shots and shots in sequence. The individual shots correspond to sentences, the sequences of shots to paragraphs. A film shot is the picture a camera takes all at one shooting. For example, the screen reveals a man's face. His hand moves into the frame to his mouth, and he removes a cigarette. This is one shot. Then his full figure appears. This is a second shot if it is "cut in" after the first shot. If the full figure had been revealed by the camera backing away from his face until it included his whole body, all this would be one shot.

A film is made by splicing together a number of shots into meaningful sequences. It is not made by starting up a camera and recording a continuous flow of scenery or action. In the film *Girl Shy,* Harold Lloyd dashes madly down the track after a train, keeping pace only a few feet from the people leaning out of the observation car. After a few seconds of his pursuit, a passenger's scarf is blown into Harold's eyes; he is blinded but keeps running. The train takes the left track at a switch, and Harold continues on the right track a hundred feet before he realizes the train has left him. All this is achieved in a sequence of short-cut shots looking over Harold's back toward the passengers, then from the train toward him, then from behind him again toward the disappearing train—medium shots and long shots projected at a speed which leaves the viewer breathless but clear about what happened. The sequence takes less than a minute. Not only is the action believable and funny but, like any first-rate piece of art, it enlarges to a symbolic level suggesting that Harold himself has become like a train switched accidentally to the wrong track—reflecting the unexpected and ironic quality that life often possesses. No words are spoken in this film sequence as it was made during the silent era. But even a modern director with sound at his disposal would probably shoot the sequence without dialogue.

For people trained in literature and stage drama, the difficulties involved in seeing films as pictures are great. We are accustomed to seeing pictures in movies, on television, and in picture magazines. Yet we are not conscious of their organization, their "cutting," or their relationship to the words that often accompany them in captions or voiced narration. Michelangelo Antonioni, a highly respected film director, reveals that he learned a great deal about the art of putting together film shots from studying comic strips—which are also essentially a series of spliced shots. Yet most of us who are knowing in literary techniques have never given a thought to the pictorial structure of a comic strip. When we leaf through the picture stories in *Life* or *Look* magazines, we are usually unconscious of the interplay of meaning between the pictures and the words accompanying them; the caption, for example, may lead us to see more or less in a picture than we would see without it.

What does it mean to say that a film is principally visual rather than verbal? We would be dishonest if we suggested that we know the full answer to that question, for the grammar of film is yet to be delineated, and pictures may never lend themselves to the precise analysis which modern grammarians have given us of verbal language.

AN AURAL MEDIUM

Although film is primarily a visual medium, sound has an important function. (The leading British film quarterly is named *Sight and Sound.*) The bubbling offbeat sounds of the magic chemical apparatus in Alexander Mackendrick's *The Man in the White Suit* give Alec Guinness' satire of modern manufacturing part of its humorous tone. The use of sound in John Huston's *The African Queen* suggests the subtle counterpoint between picture and sound striven for in some motion pictures. It opens with its title and credits superimposed on a picture of deep African river banks pushing their way at the viewer as the camera moves up the river in a boat, while a loud series of animal sounds and cries prepares the viewer for the exotic world that is to come. Although most filmgoers may not be consciously aware of film techniques, they are guided and prepared by them or sometimes confused. In *The African*

Queen, when Katherine Hepburn and Humphrey Bogart step into the boat to flee the settlement from the Germans, the music is portentous, stock signal for thrill and fear. Yet a few moments later it unaccountably shifts to a light bouncing melody as the boat glides down the jungle river. The music at first suggests the peril of the departure; the music that follows perhaps implies that even amid this danger the missionary's daughter will find some pleasant companionship with the rough trader. A tension between civilization and rawness pervades the film, but it is questionable whether the music succeeds in supporting and suggesting this subtle interplay. Such delicate syncopations of picture and sound require an artistic control of the first order from the film director and his many co-workers.

SIMULTANEOUS COMMUNICATION

A picture of people or objects in the real world is more complete and particular than a sentence, and a film director can communicate in no smaller units than single pictures. He may focus in close-up on a small object, say a ring on a man's finger, but it must be that ring on that finger, unique and particular. The shot of the ring is more specific than the word *ring,* which by itself is a generalization referring to a round object which may enclose or slip onto other objects, or to a noise, or to an action. The sentence "He put the ring on her finger" is highly generalized in comparison with a shot of a hand slipping a ring on a finger. Or to take another example: in language, the verb *tied* suggests only generally a relationship, not specifying whether the tie is made with silk thread or rope, accomplished tightly or loosely, or through force or love. A film shot of objects or people *tied* introduces simultaneously people, objects, and the relationship between them, as well as the materials used in tying and a suggestion of the manner in which the tying was accomplished. As Marshall McLuhan of the University of Toronto would say, the picture shows us many things at once, in one instantaneous communication, whereas the reading of words and sentences in their sequence builds meanings cumulatively. The picture provides simultaneous communication while type, typography, provides "linear" communication.

Film employs strategies which may be likened to literary strategies—simile and metaphor, symbolism, and irony. If we are to judge the worth of a film, we must see how these strategies are practiced visually before we can assess their artistic quality.

SIMILE AND METAPHOR

In a film, a nervous, fussy, quick-gaited man hurries along the beach. In the next shot a sandpiper minces along the wet sand. We have been shown that the man is like a sandpiper. The sequence of two shots creates a film simile. In another sequence a man lies in bed, eyes closed. The next shot shows him, like T. S. Eliot's J. Alfred Prufrock, watching mermaids "riding seaward on the waves." The same man has lain on the bed in one shot and lingered in caves by the sea in the next, with no transition. The sequence creates a film metaphor. Although the director may ordinarily use dissolves to show the melting or fusion of two events in time, he may occasionally dissolve one picture into another so that a man "becomes" metaphorically the animal or object which is seen next on the screen.

SYMBOLISM

As in literature, a film simile or metaphor may rise to the height of symbolism, pointing to wider meanings on another

The sea and the bleak rocks form a harsh background for the adults struggling for communication in *L'Avventura*.

level. In Otto Preminger's *Advise and Consent,* Henry Fonda, the nominee for Secretary of State, under attack for lying to an investigating committee, is shown telling the truth about himself to his son. The next shot reveals the Senator, who is heading the committee investigating the Secretary, embracing his child at his home. The juxtaposition of these shots creates an analogy which not only neatly shows that these two men are alike in one way but also suggests that all men are human, with deepfelt ties, even though they may be in conflict.

In Michelangelo Antonioni's *L'Avventura,* the symbol of human alienation and loneliness comes not through a verbal image but through the whole first twenty-five minutes of pictures of people individually, or in pairs, picking their way along the jagged face of a great rock island in the Mediterranean, losing sight of one another, moving apparently aimlessly in what is a search for a girl who has disappeared from them, perhaps into the sea. The rocky surface, washed by a sea, is sharp as death and lovely as life—at one moment breathtaking in beauty and the next chilling in ferocity as it lashes the inlets where there is no chance for boat or man to come. ashore safely.

The director does not present a popular magazine story, slick on the surface, open and empty. He asks the viewer to read his pictures on many levels, always including the literal and the symbolic. In John Ford's *The Grapes of Wrath,* the rickety piled-high truck in which the Joads carry all their family possessions hits the steep shoulder of the road, teeters crazily, and rights itself. This brief action symbolizes the precariousness of the family's economic condition, of the whole trip to California, and of the country's economy during the depression.

The silent comedies of Charlie Chaplin, Harold Lloyd, and Buster Keaton, like Shakespeare's plays, speak on several levels of sophistication and understanding, including the symbolic. The pratfall and the kick in the pants, elaborated again and again with brilliant variations, are funny on the first level and ramify to wider psychological experience on the second. Kicking the cop in the pants releases everyman's hostile feelings toward authority. It is the smirking, superior character who gets the final, most ignominious pie in the face. Life's way of letting everyman down is dramatized in a brief sequence in Harold Lloyd's series of herculean attempts in *Girl Shy* to reach his girl before she marries the wrong man. Reduced to walking, he attempts to hitch a ride. Several cars roar by without pausing. He finds a paper bag by the roadside and pops it as a car passes. The prissy old driver stops to look for a flat tire. When the car starts up again, Harold jumps on the back and the driver immediately turns into his own driveway and stops. The audience recognizes in a burst of laughter that this is the way life goes. The film makers have accomplished this symbolic comment on life without the use of words.

IRONY

Good films, like good literature, are filled with ironies. In the silent comedy the ironies may be quick and open; in today's best films they may be partially hidden, making considerable demands on the viewer. The filmgoer who has not habituated himself to looking at motion pictures as statements primarily visual may sense visual irony at the time he witnesses it but never be able to articulate it when speaking of the film to others. A simple but powerful irony is projected in Fred Zinnemann's *The Search,* where the American soldier, Montgomery Clift, attempts to share his lunch with a war orphan scrounging amid the ruins of a city. Upon being offered a sandwich, the boy retreats. The soldier throws half a sandwich to him and he gobbles it. Then Clift places the other half on the ground and drives off. In this short succession of shots, Director Zinnemann presents the paradox of a starved boy so fearful he will not eat when first offered food. With the same pictures he establishes the accepting, sympathetic character of the soldier.

Film, like the stage, may reveal dramatic irony in which the audience knows what the actor does not. This irony is often communicated through pictures rather than dialogue. For example, in *Movie Crazy,* Harold Lloyd seeks a meeting with the girl he idolizes. She refuses to see him, writing a note of rejection which she gives to a friend to deliver to Harold, who is waiting at the door. He is overjoyed to receive the note. The camera looks up at him standing on the top step reading and shows the girl's handwriting on the *under* side of the note paper. Harold smiles ecstatically as he reads the *top* side, which reveals itself in close-up as a formal invitation to a dinner dance. No words are spoken; the audience pauses a second and then breaks into laughter as it discerns the irony.

CLICHÉ

If we are to see films as perceptively as we see the stage production of *Death of a Salesman* or *Hamlet,* we must not only come to see how film exploits visual and aural techniques but also perceive whether those techniques are being applied creatively or tritely. At the far end of the scale stands the travelogue which bids goodbye to the South Sea island in the fading red and yellow sunset. At the opposite end of the scale stands a picture like François Truffaut's *The Four Hundred Blows,* in which two children, bereft of adult attention and love, walk a kind of dance throughout the picture along the streets of Paris to the tune of music that seems to come bouncingly from a carousel—implying their imminent separation from society. They are not cute in their walk; they are cocksure boys who imitate adults' manners. They are not menacing in their swagger, but they grow steadily surer in their movements as they cross the boundaries of convention and law. In contrast to their fresh and convincing quality is the cliché-filled characterization of a sympathetic young girl played by Hayley Mills in Bryan Forbes' *Whistle Down the Wind.* She is all sugar instead of compassion; she speaks flatly those lines which reveal that she understands other children, but she seldom *looks* as if she understands. Yet her little brother, who speaks with a vocal difficulty that might make him a stereotyped and sentimental little tyke, moves with devastating originality.

Such examples of cliché and freshness in film belong to the stage as well as to the motion picture, for they involve simply the way actors move and talk. In many film sequences in silent comedies, actions occur that could not be realized on stage. In the great moments in the films of Charlie Chaplin, W. C. Fields, Laurel and Hardy, and Harold Lloyd, we often see what we think is going to be a cliché explode before our eyes. In the film short, *The Boat,* Buster Keaton throws the anchor out of his boat with an authoritative and energetic heave. It floats. As one sequence in a series of attempts to commit suicide, the disappointed lover Harold Lloyd rushes up a bridge to a park lagoon, ties a weight around his neck, and throws himself heroically off the bridge. He lands feet first in eighteen inches of water. In Denis and Terry Sanders' film *War Hunt,* the viewer sees an attack of North Koreans on American troops that avoids all the battle clichés of the hundreds of war films that have preceded it. The waves of North Koreans come on in the almost blinding light, not in stereotyped close-ups of leering "Oriental evil" but in medium shots (middle distance) of individual men stumbling forward, their faces hard to make out, their coverall uniforms and long-billed caps making them look like bulky American garage mechanics and in that look, presenting to the viewer, who sits in the trench with the American soldiers, a truer and more fearsome sight than he has ever seen in a war movie. In these sequences by the Sanders brothers and Keaton and Lloyd, the viewer is treated with fresh visualizations of common actions. More often in film such actions are presented tritely. For example, sexual experience is seldom shown in American films except in the stereotyped shot of a kiss or by shots of flames leaping in a fireplace or waves breaking on the shore, instead of being suggested in ways that are not trite.

DIALOGUE

Although film moves first of all visually, it is also verbal —actors speak words, and frequently an off-camera voice narrates or explains. Like the dialogue of a play, the dialogue of a film is stripped down, without such editorial comment as "He said, angrily." But its starkness must be even more severe than that of the stage play. If the stage actor holds in his hand a small object, like a gun whose rifling is the subject of conversation, he must describe it to the audience; he has no close-up camera. The dialogue of a film, on the other hand, must be spare in description of objects, because usually the camera shows the objects, and talk about them would be redundant and unrealistic. In life we describe in detail the facade of a building we are showing to a friend, although we may make judgments about it, saying, "Isn't it beautiful, the way the lines of the windows are repeated?" In a skillful film, the camera shows the repeating lines of windows and the actor says, "Isn't that beautiful?" or nothing at all.

STYLE

Principally because of the close-up, film actors must learn to project feelings with restraint. In silent films, the movement, obviously, was all-important—in comedy, often a caricature of real-life movement, consequently supercharged with meaning. For those who could not read the subtitles giving the dialogue, the actors in dramatic films exaggerated actions and often employed stereotyped gestures and movements to suggest what they were saying. But since the advent of sound, film acting has become a more subtle visual art. Actors have learned that they need master, not a fine stage diction and an ability to project their voices to the last balcony, but rather a natural way of talking and the look of life as seen from four-foot conversational distance. Television-trained actors are frequently more accomplished in film than stage-trained actors, and film actors are often bad on the stage. Richard Basehart, who brilliantly and often wordlessly portrayed the man who befriended the little girl in Federico Fellini's film *La Strada,* received this response from *The New York Times'* Arthur Gelb for his stage performance of Richard II: ". . . his final, self-analytical speeches are delivered with unemotional monotony. . . . Oddly enough, while Mr. Basehart is among the best in a dubiously equipped cast, he is also the least audible. Many of his lines are swallowed and thrown away unheard." (June 18, 1962)

American filmgoers know and appreciate the careless, natural movements brought to the screen by actors like Marlon Brando in *On the Waterfront* and Montgomery Clift in *The Search.* They delight in the tippy-toe walk of Jacques Tati in *Mr. Hulot's Holiday,* and in the utterly original and true walk of Piper Laurie as the cripple, or the assured movements of Jackie Gleason as the pool champion, both in Robert Rossen's *The Hustler.* When Albert Finney rides his bike through the narrow streets of the factory town in *Saturday Night and Sunday Morning,* he conveys a wide range of feelings without saying a word. The fact that television is now supplying actors to Hollywood and that silent comedies exhibiting the great masters of movement are being revived suggests that film actors are artists—some good, some bad, but artists.

ECONOMY

Speaking of the art of painting, Samuel Butler, the author of *The Way of All Flesh,* said: "The first step towards taming the eyes is to teach them not to see too much." This kind of economy is manifest throughout François Truffaut's film *The Four Hundred Blows.* In the correction center for children, Jean Pierre Leaud, as the child, snatches a piece of bread before the meal has formally begun in the inmates' dining hall. An attendant appears before him, asks "Right or left?" Jean Pierre says, "Left." The attendant removes the watch from his own wrist and hits the boy hard in the face with his left hand. The ritual has been recorded and consequently the spirit of the place established in a few seconds of film.

Employing economy in a different way, Truffaut points

up the impersonality of the correction center by presenting the psychiatrist's long interview with Jean Pierre without ever giving the viewer a look at the psychiatrist. The viewer hears the doctor's voice but sees only Jean Pierre's face, alternating between expressions of winking understanding of the adult world and regret for his life without affection.

UNITIES

The unities of *The Four Hundred Blows,* as in any first-rate work of art, are achieved on many levels. The artistic tone of this story of parental failure and youthful catastrophe is restraint. Mother and father live under strain, she having her affairs and he complaining. The father does not understand or know his son as deeply as he should, but he speaks to him as an equal and loves him. The mother generally considers the boy a brat, a person in the way, but there are moments when she too displays affection. At an early point in the film, when Jean Pierre, at the height of his rebellion against school and society, burns an offering to Balzac, his self-appointed patron saint, and almost sets the apartment on fire, the parents break down in sympathy and go off with him to a movie, reuniting themselves as a family for a golden moment. Throughout the film, Jean Pierre and his school chum move and talk like boys, never long despondent, light and childlike in manner even in their too-adult reactions, such as Jean Pierre's short-blurted laugh at his father's insistence that his mother really loves him. The point of the film emerges: you and I are no less cruel as parents, and our child is perhaps just as purposelessly moving toward complete alienation from society.

At the end of *The Four Hundred Blows,* when Jean Pierre has escaped the correction center and run for miles toward the sea, his feet making tracks in the wet sand, he enters the shallow water. As he turns back and looks at the camera, the moving picture freezes to a still photograph, with his slightly opened mouth caught in an expression of questioning. Then the camera moves in closer on this still face and the film ends. The viewer walks out of the theatre reflecting on the ambiguity: was the boy going to stride into the sea to his death? Or did his turning signify he had decided to return to the world? Whatever the answer, the viewer has no doubt about whom the look was intended for—the boy was looking at him, at all of us who have created his desolate world.

THEME

As a great film director creates great ambiguities, so too he takes up great themes. He examines the significant experiences of man's struggle, as Alain Resnais examined the roots and fact and consequences of nuclear warfare in *Hiroshima, Mon Amour;* as Orson Welles studied the ego-structure of a tycoon in *Citizen Kane;* as Tony Richardson examined the conflicts of adolescence with the adult world in *A Taste of Honey* and *The Loneliness of the Long Distance Runner;* as Robert Rossen examined the nature of demagoguery in *All the King's Men;* as Delbert Mann examined the incoherence and loneliness of an average man and woman in *Marty.*

CHAPTER TWO

The Conscious Stream

CONTINUITY

The film is a series of movements, a stream of moving pictures which comes at the viewer, one appearing to emerge from behind the other, the preceding picture appearing to vanish instantaneously into the space between the viewer and the screen—not to have moved left or right and then out of the range of his vision. This stream of shots carries movement not only within the individual shot (as the hero vaults on his horse) but also from shot to shot (one shot: the villain hides behind the rocks; next shot: the hero rides toward him, unsuspecting).

This stream of pictures, which is the essence of film, is by its nature hard to apprehend. It rushes by, and we seldom can recall the order of shots that composed it any more than we can recall the order of all our movements this morning as we scrambled two eggs and toasted a slice of bread. If we are to know the order of "shots" in life or in the movie theatre, we must keep a running notation of them, and by such notations we are already beginning to perceive arrangements and to find meaning.

Communication by print is more easily analyzed; it is there on the page to be returned to again and again. But the conscious stream of pictures in film is like the stream of tone and time in music—difficult for the layman to recall. For most persons a transcription of musical notes on paper is necessary if they are to analyze music they have heard. Most of us are not used to listening to music and watching film in such a way that we can talk about their structure and order.

Two devices may help us to sense the conscious stream in film. One is to see an amateurish home movie and reflect upon the relationship of one shot to the next. Perhaps we are shown some yellow mountain wildflowers against the blue sky above the Rockies. Then suddenly an elbow dominates the picture, and Momma moves onto the screen in her blue swimsuit with yellow stripes. Next we see a smiling Canadian Royal Mounted policeman, resplendent in red, mounted on his arrogant horse. Is the film trying to say that Mother in her swimsuit is like flowers in the Rockies and that her beauty stirred the smile on the Mountie's face? This sequence might be slyly commenting on the unromantic figure Mother cuts in her old swimsuit, but then what is the flailing elbow doing there? As we are jerked from one shot to the next without transition or meaningful contrast, we can only conclude that the sequence is random, ineptly edited, and hence meaningless. It is not art.

DISCONTINUITY

Another way to point up the nature of the flow in film is to consider literary works which approach film in their form, for example, the writings of James Joyce, Marcel Proust, Franz Kafka, Virginia Woolf, or John Dos Passos. A useful story to consider is "The Secret Life of Walter Mitty," by James Thurber, which achieves its remarkable concentration by a stream of filmlike discontinuous "shots." As written, the story opens with the Commander of a Navy hydroplane ordering his crew to speed up the engines to fly through hurricane weather. The next shot presents Mrs. Mitty telling her husband that he should not drive so fast. She leaves him in the car, admonishing him to wear gloves. He puts the gloves on, takes them off, and puts them on again. He drives past a hospital; the next shot reveals him removing his surgeon's gloves.

He accepts the challenge of operating when other doctors falter, and the sequence ends with the phrase "nurses handed him shining . . ." The three dots of the ellipsis signify a fadeout.

In Thurber's next shot an insolent parking lot attendant shouts, "Back it up, Mac!" After yielding his car to the attendant, Mitty walks along Main Street dreaming of the time (flashback) he inadvertently got the chains of his car wound around the axle. He remembers to buy the overshoes his wife ordered him to get; and as he thinks of other shopping duties, a newsboy goes by "shouting something about the Waterbury trial." In the next shot the District Attorney is shoving before Mitty a heavy Webley-Vickers automatic pistol. At the culmination of a series of melodramatics in the courtroom, the District Attorney strikes at the girl who has fallen into Mitty's arms. Mitty hits the attorney on the chin, saying, "You miserable cur!" . . . (dissolve). The next shot presents Mitty saying "puppy biscuit" as he walks down the street. Entering the A & P, he asks for a special brand of puppy biscuit.

At this point the typography indicates by extra space between paragraphs a major break in the story. The new paragraph presents Mitty looking at his watch and thinking that his wife would be "through at the hairdresser's in fifteen minutes." He picks up an old copy of *Liberty* and looks at pictures of bombers. Three dots indicate a dissolve, and the sergeant is saying to Captain Mitty that one of their fellow aviators is unfit for combat. Mitty casually insists that he will go up and fight the enemy. He straps on his Webley-Vickers automatic, turns and waves to the sergeant, saying "Cheerio" (dissolve). In the next shot something strikes his shoulder. It is Mrs. Mitty finding him in the hotel. A few minutes later when she stops at the corner to get something at the drugstore, Mitty leans against the wall, smoking (dissolve). He puts his shoulders back and refuses the handkerchief, facing the firing squad alone and "inscrutable to the last."

"The Secret Life of Walter Mitty" is presented in words which our mind converts to images. These closely approximate the conscious stream of film. The story is nothing like a continuous narrative. The movement from one shot or sequence to another sometimes is broken and sometimes clearly tied. The tie between the first two sequences consists of the emphasis on speeding. The Commander says, "Rev her up to 8,500!" and Mrs. Mitty says, "Not so fast!" These two statements placed next to each other require the reader to connect them in some meaningful way, just as a series of apparently disparate images in a poem may require the reader to make connections, for example in T. S. Eliot's line from "The Hollow Men": "Rat's coat, crowskin, crossed staves." At another point in "The Secret Life of Walter Mitty" the tie is achieved by the use of different words with the same references: "miserable cur" and "puppy biscuit." The essential technique of this story—so unlike conventional narration—is *break,* from one shot to another. In film this technique is called *cutting.* If Thurber's story or a professional film were made of nothing but quick cuts—abrupt transitions from one event to another —the effect would be disastrous to the reader or viewer. Like a good film maker, James Thurber has avoided real discontinuity by the repetition of a number of ideas and objects, which hold the shots together by a subtle but important thread. Thurber ties the discontinuous elements by repeating the same word or mentioning the same object in several sequences. The cylinders of the Navy hydroplane go "ta-pocketa-pocketa-pocketa-pocketa-pocketa"; the anesthetizer in the hospital goes "pocketa-pocketa-queep-pocketa-queep"; the flame throwers heard by the Air Force captain go "pocketa-pocketa-pocketa." Mrs. Mitty suggests that Mitty should visit Dr. Renshaw because of his nervousness. When Mitty becomes the doctor in the operating room, he is introduced to a Dr. Renshaw. Thinking of his embarrassment at getting the chains wound round the axle of his car, Mitty says, "I'll wear my right arm in a sling. They won't grin at me then." Later in the courtroom Mitty's attorney shouts, "We have shown that he wore his right arm in a sling on the night of the fourteenth of July" (and therefore could not have fired the shot).

Likewise with the skillfully made motion picture, the shots and sequences are usually discontinuous. The shock of their coming one after another is part of the power of film. But they do not come so disconnectedly that they confuse the viewer.

Through many devices—sound effect, picture, and dialogue—the competent director spins his connecting thread. So much is movement in film that something must act as an anchor. On the simplest level a visual anchor may be provided by the repetition of or centering upon an object or person. *The Four Hundred Blows* opens with the streets of Paris seen from a moving car. The barren black trees and gray buildings sweep by at an almost dizzying pace, but beyond the lowest buildings and occasionally down the vista of a side street we see again and again the Eiffel Tower which is the anchor of this ride. Its recurring presence allows the viewer both to sense the motion, because the distant tower seems the only thing in the landscape not moving, and to endure the motion, because the tower is his familiar and stationary security.

On a somewhat more complex plane is a sequence of shots near the beginning of an otherwise uninspired film. As the incoming class of recent medical graduates arrives at a large city hospital for their first day of duty, the camera examines each one and watches him turn toward the tower hospital building and give it his first look of awe and wonderment. Each new resident so inspects this building, the real place of his next year's residence and the symbol of his coming career. The camera looks at the hospital over the shoulder of these persons, seeing it from different views—from front, side, and rear. It is a different building to each—as it should be— yet imposing and perhaps frightening to all. The sequence suggests the individuality of each intern; the hospital, although seen each time from a different angle, remains its monolithic self.

On a still more complex level is the domination of the face, figure, or name of Charles Kane in Orson Welles' *Citizen Kane*. The film proceeds by a recalling of Kane's life through the memories of his friends and companions. In that sense the picture is composed of a series of disparate stories, but visually it is held together by the repetition of Kane's presence, either his face, his figure, or his name, directly or in shots of photographs of him. When a financier goes to the farm to pick up the boy Charles Kane and bring him to the city, he talks to Charles' parents. Through a window, we see Charles playing in the snow. When Kane is reveling in a banquet celebration and the camera moves away from his figure to inspect the crowd and the chorus girls, Kane's figure is reflected in a dark window in the center of the screen. Frequently in the film when someone is talking about Kane, a picture of Kane dominates the room. So in this film even when the protagonist is not actually in the foreground of a shot, he often appears in reflection or image of one kind or another. By repetition the film drums Kane at us, much as Hitler or Stalin drummed their images at their people.

In a motion picture the conscious stream may be weak, mediocre, or brilliant in composition. In the trial scene in the film *The Devil's Disciple,* where Kirk Douglas, as Dick Dudgeon impersonating the Reverend Anderson, and Sir Laurence Olivier as Gentleman Johnny, the presiding general, speak Bernard Shaw's dialogue, the sequence simply cuts from one person to the other and back without exploitation of film's marvelous ability to move in two ways—within the frame or from shot to shot. Shaw's dialogue is so brilliant that it can carry the story by itself. In these sequences, the film proceeds by words more than by the conscious stream of pictures and is thus less filmic than such a motion picture as Olivier's

Name, image, and gesture, all overpowering, reinforce this shot of Orson Wells, as the demagogic Kane in *Citizen Kane*.

Henry V, where the long soliloquy before the Battle of Agincourt is given special illumination and an intensified meaning by the camera which moves meditatively, now turning to the king's intent face, now to the low camp fires, now to the men's apprehensive forms, reinforcing the voice.

In *The Search,* the sequence of an orphaned boy's dreaming of finding his mother is carefully arranged and the shots adroitly spliced together. The boy is a derelict of World War II who has been cared for by an American soldier. The sequence is made of this stream of shots: the boy's face is seen in close-up, his hand and arm covering part of his face, emphasizing what is left to the viewer—his remarkable, plaintive eyes. The next close-up shows his hand idly drawing horizontal lines on a piece of paper. When he begins crossing them with vertical lines, he looks down, frightened at what he has created. The next shot dissolves to a wire fence against the sky which repeats the cross-hatched design. The camera pans down to reveal people behind the fence holding out their hands in supplication. He sees his mother among them, moves forward to kiss her through the wire. She is torn away from him. Back in the room where he was drawing, he jumps from his chair and runs downstairs. He sneaks out the door and runs off to a real wire fence where he watches adults walk by, scanning them for his mother, whom he does not find. Again he runs off, ending his flight on a country hillside where he waddles weakly up the slope to stand in broken frustration between two birches. His soldier friend finds him. "Hello," he says to the boy, who moves away. "Hey! Don't run." The boy turns and moves into the soldier's arms.

This consciously created stream builds its tension and achieves its release with filmic strength and economy. It tells a great deal about the boy's relationship to his mother and the soldier and about the effect of war upon him, all in three and one-half minutes. Carried out crudely, such a sequence might be disconcerting to the viewer. He might sense the symbolism of the crossed lines but fail to understand why he was seeing them repeated at various moments in the sequence. The story might have broken down visually. But Director Zinnemann gives the viewer clues to hold together the stream of disparate shots. The boy's preoccupation with past imprisonment is shown by his doodling the lines of a fence on paper. The quick cut to the fence where he meets his mother omits the film's conventional signs of exit from a building. No movement toward or through a door is shown, and therefore the viewer infers that the shot of son and mother meeting is daydream. The whole sequence, as traced earlier above, projects complex and ambivalent feelings—the boy's fear of fences as symbols of harshness and captivity, their attraction for him as reminders of his last knowledge of his mother. The conscious stream shows his dream of rejoining her, the hard reality of the loss which he must accept, his rejection of the soldier who is his new mother-figure, and his ultimate reacceptance of the soldier. In its flow, such a stream is analogous to music, a medium that proceeds by tone and time.

CONTEXT

What can be accomplished by the selection and ordering of shots in a film sequence is astounding. The Russian director V. I. Pudovkin tells of editing one picture of a man's face into three sequences.[1] In the first, the face was followed by a shot of a plate of soup on a table. In the second, the face was followed by a shot of a coffin containing a dead woman. In the third, the face was followed by a shot of a girl playing with a humorous looking toy bear. The viewers who saw the sequences praised the actor for "the heavy pensiveness of his mood over the forgotten soup," the sorrow with which he looked at the coffin, and the happy smile with which he

[1] V. I. Pudovkin, *Film Technique and Film Acting* (New York, Lear, 1949), p. 140.

The Search

Seated alone in the soldier's room, the boy begins to draw.

Idly, his hand draws cross-hatching on the paper.

The design stirs his memory, and

the drawing begins to fade, and slowly dissolves

the grim fencing of a prison stockade.

In his memory, the boy again kisses his mother goodbye. (The hat seen here is an important visual detail, linking the past and present.)

He remembers that the compound in which he is presently located also has such a fence. He leaves the room, goes downstairs, and outside,

to stare at the line of refugees entering, as he looks for his mother.

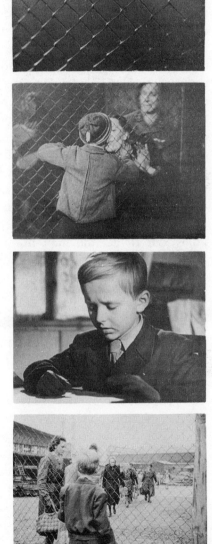

25

looked at the girl and her toy bear. Yet in every sequence the same shot of his face was used. Nothing could more sharply point up the fact that the motion picture is a series of discontinuous shots artfully strung together. They flow because they come one after another from the same source, not because the camera eye presents the same visual flow we experience in real life, where we move from one room or person to another through a landscape total in context. It is true that we select out of any landscape what we want to see or what demands our attention, but we live through wide-angled eyes that are with us all our waking hours. No editor cuts out pieces of our journey, showing us the door through which we will exit and then the lake one hundred yards from the house. In this sense our experience is not telescoped. It is not composed of discrete bits of visual experience which flow into each other only because they are juxtaposed or, more accurately, placed one behind the other and projected at us. The simplest act, like going out to get the mail in the morning, if photographed completely, would take up too much time in a film, just as the writer would take up too much space in a novel if he described every movement of the body involved and every wall and rug and patch of ground encountered by the man going to get the mail. Only if the act is highly significant to the total story would a good film maker present it visually in its entirety. The art of film making, like any other art, is in large part the art of omitting the nonessential.

The viewer of films may understandably complain that motion pictures come too fast for him to see the art behind the conscious stream. He cannot slow down his look, as he does when he reads a line of poetry, and read it again and again. Film analysis requires several seeings of the same sequence and usually notetaking. But once a person has looked at a film twice and thereby freed himself from the story line so that he can study the technique of putting together shots (what is called "editing"), then he sees the next motion picture with heightened awareness of its filmic accomplishments or failures. If a film is being shown in a classroom or special viewing room (privately, in a sense) and the projector is equipped with a reverse switch, a student may stop the film upon second showing and play back several times a sequence that merits study. To examine a current commercial film closely, he may need to visit the theatre twice.

The process of learning to "read" film may be better understood by reminding readers of literature how they developed their sensitivity to sound effects in writing. When they began reading, they could appreciate only crude rhymes and blatant rhythmic effects such as those of Kipling's "Boots, boots, boots, boots." But after study and restudy of masters of sound in writing, they were able to appreciate upon first reading such sounds as Frost's "The only other sound's the sweep/ Of easy wind and downy flake," or such subtleties as Wallace Stevens' line from "Peter Quince at the Clavier": "So evenings die, in their green going."

In *The Search,* the soldier who befriends the boy listens as a fellow soldier describes the difficulties involved in taking the boy back to the United States. The soldier explains the red tape involved, citing one requirement after another, emphasizing each with a hard gesture of his hand. As his voice continues hammering out the necessary steps, a close-up of the boy's expression appears, puzzled and helpless. The overlaying of the words upon the boy's face (although seen for only three seconds) strengthens the meaning of both shots and suggests ultimately to the viewer how exquisitely wrong are the methods of bureaucracies for dealing with human beings. Only two shots—and dialogue ironically supported by the feeling in the boy's face—make up this segment of the stream, short but significant and easy to follow.

Part of the power of this sequence of two shots lies in the ability of the boy's face to project meaning by itself. His eyes are pleading or haunting, his face betrays helplessness or the look of a child who has become adult before his time. He was undoubtedly chosen for this film because he could project so much with his face and total physical appearance, not because he could read lines with versatility and precision, like a stage actor. A person trained to appreciate stage acting might consider these capacities trivial—and in a sense they are, for they do not represent skill as much as inherited physiognomy —but such visual power is at the heart of film, and in the total context of film making it must be a major, not minor consideration.

Throughout *The Search,* this little boy's responsive face carries along much of the movement of sequences. Asked questions, he frequently speaks no words, but his face says all. In daily life persons trained in literature may forget how much meaning comes to them from the expressions of faces; the film maker forgets this at his peril. The power of facial expression may seem remote from the process of ordering shots into filmic sequences, but it is discussed here to point up the interconnectedness of all aspects of film making. All the visual and aural methods of telling a story or revealing life must be joined symphonically in creating a good film.

So far are most filmgoers from sensing the nature of this symphony that when they want to comment upon something other than the story in a film they fall back upon the often meaningless phrase "camera work." As the next chapters will point out, the angle of the camera, the way it travels, and the composition of black and white (or color) forms within the frame are all parts of the symphony, but the conscious stream remains the center of the motion picture.

One simple expedient will allow a viewer of film to begin to see the conscious stream more clearly, that is for him to watch one shot—say a man walking out a door—and as he watches, ask himself, "What shot will come next?" This stratagem will enable him to sense the contrast or similarity between the shot that follows and the shot he has just seen. He will begin to see the flow. When the viewer is caught and held by a good film, he cannot so disengage himself to study its editing, and no one wants consciousness of art to nullify the experience of art. However, this technique of anticipating the next shot is as necessary to understanding the art of film as studying a sentence of prose or a line of poetry is to the understanding of literary craft. The analysis usually comes after the first reading, but it must come at some time if one is to improve his sensibilities.

CHAPTER THREE

To See,
Feelingly

LEAR. O, ho, are you there with me? No eyes in your
head, nor no money in your purse? Your eyes are in a heavy
case; your purse in a light: yet you see how this world goes.
GLOSTER. I see it feelingly.
King Lear, Act IV, Scene 6

POINT OF VIEW

Film is art. All art is a fight against chaos;[1] reality as we
know it is chaotic, disparate, and meaningless until our intelli-
gence and sensibility can impose some order on it. The eye at
work in daily experience is involved in a never-ending process
of selection or rejection, of putting together or perceiving connections and relationships. The artist creates his own reality,
selecting, ordering, making analogies, and finding meaning.
Our own uncertain age finds old truths crumbling in this uni-
verse, and old values no longer sustaining us. Much of what
we call modern art professes a reality incomprehensible to us
and somehow disturbing, private, and anarchical.

The artist's eye is like our own but rendered more capable, by virtue of a superior sensitivity, of seeing order in chaos,
and of rendering it in terms of images. As Theseus says in *A
Midsummer Night's Dream,* it glances

[1] Arnold Hauser, *The Social History of Art* (New York, Knopf, 1951),
quoted in Daniel Talbot (ed.), *Film: An Anthology* (New York, Simon and
Schuster, 1959), p. 70.

. . . from heaven to earth, from earth to heaven;
And as imagination bodies forth
The forms of things unknown, the poet's pen
Turns them to shapes, and gives to airy nothing
A local habitation and a name.

The camera eye is a poet's eye; the moving picture, as Susanne Langer points out, is a poetic mode.[2] It is a poetic mode because, whether we are aware of the presence of the camera or not, it is there—usually unobtrusively calling our attention to this object or that person, or to an expression or a detail, controlling our perceptions, establishing mood, making connections between things, forming our attitudes. The director expresses his sensibility in terms of images selected and ordered perhaps on the set or during the editing. The point of view may be the director's; it may be that of some character involved in the action or on the periphery of the action. It is always rendered in terms of images and their relationship to one another, and the relationship is specifically temporal, spatial, causal, or so invested with meaning as to be symbolic.

The term "point of view" has two distinct implications. The primary one concerns the physical location of the camera. The second implication has to do with the way in which the position of the camera helps to reveal the attitude of the observer, or director and hence to influence our own. The ultimate result of the selection of a point of view is to establish meaning.

THE CAMERA EYE

Only occasionally, and in the most "flat" transcription of action, is the camera static. For the most part it is constantly

[2] Susanne Langer, *Feeling and Form* (New York, Scribner, 1953), p. 411.

changing location. It may establish a locale and a perspective by means of a long shot; it may move in for a close examination of a detail or an expression; it may switch from one to another of persons participating in action or dialogue; it may hover over an action; it may follow a scene from a vantage point above, or below; it may, in addition, assume some of the prerogatives of a conscious observer, and by means of forcing our attention on an object, or suddenly juxtaposing one object against another, invest them with meaning. By means of a change of focus or a blurring of the outlines, it may suggest distortion of vision common to a person whose own sensibilities are confused by emotion, memory, or neurosis.

The opening scenes of many well-known novels correspond to the establishing shots of the camera at the beginning of a film. (This is not to say that if these novels were rendered into film—many have been—these opening scenes should necessarily be translated into visual introductions on the part of the camera.) The purpose of an introductory scene, whether chapter or long shot, remains the same: to identify the place, to suggest its importance in the events which are to follow, to introduce the main character or characters, to suggest the nature of the conflict, and to state the underlying theme.

The opening chapter of *Great Expectations* is primarily visual. We hover over the marshes, so to speak. The first paragraphs immediately identify Pip, the protagonist whose formation and "expectations" will provide the raw material of the story, in the act of inspecting the tombstones of his father, mother, and five little brothers. The next paragraph is panoramic:

> Ours was the marsh country, down by the river, within, as the river wound, twenty miles of the sea. My first most vivid and broad impression of the identity of things seems to me to have been gained on a memorable raw afternoon towards evening. At such a time I found out for certain, that this bleak

place overgrown with nettles was the churchyard . . .; and
that the dark flat wilderness beyond the churchyard, inter-
sected with dykes and mounts and gates, with scattered cattle
feeding on it, was the marshes; and that the low leaden line
beyond was the river; and that the distant savage lair from
which the wind was rushing, was the sea; and that the small
bundle of shivers growing afraid of it all and beginning to cry
was Pip.

Setting, mood, the identity (and pathos) of the central
character, as yet unformed (hence the name pip, or seed), the
marsh, the graveyard, and the ominous foreshadowing of river
and sea, together form a series of images which flash across
our own mind-screen—all the essentials have been introduced
in the first person narration. Those who have seen David
Lean's *Great Expectations* will never forget the extraordinary
effect of the figure of the convict, rising like a Titan from
behind the gravestone, towering over Pip, gross and menacing.
The shot in the movie was taken from Pip's point of view; the
menace of the convict looms enormous as his shadow hangs
over the whole story. The camera is low, shooting upward and
has spun around in a frightened blur to reveal the figure. The
same effect has been accomplished visually (and symbolically)
as is done a little later in the narration in the book:

> The man, after looking at me for a moment, turned me
> upside down, and emptied my pockets. There was nothing in
> them but a piece of bread. When the church came to itself—
> for he was so sudden and strong that he made it go head over
> heels before me, and I saw the steeple under my feet—when
> the church came to itself, I say, I was seated on a high tomb-
> stone, trembling, while he ate the bread ravenously.

Whereas Pip's story is told in the first person, Hardy's
The Return of the Native is told from the point of view of an
omniscient observer, whose description of Egdon Heath, the

"face on which time has made little impression," appears at first as if at an immense distance. The sky and the horizon hang over the heath, which appears as melancholy, gloomy, and lonely. No human being appears.

Countless other examples from novels will come to mind, from the opening paragraphs of *Moby Dick,* where Ishmael's eye sees everything in terms of images preoccupied with melancholia, coffins, and death, to the opening chapters of Hemingway's *A Farewell to Arms,* in which the narrator, as yet unknown to us, looks across the river and plain to the mountain; no details are given beyond the subjective and impersonal terms dry, white, cool, and brown.

Not the details, necessarily—for the important characteristic of the Hemingway opening is the absence of sharp detail, consistent with the narrator's lack of involvement—but rather the overview, the establishment of the relationship of the narrator to his surroundings, is of concern here. In the moving picture, the camera, at a distance, has the responsibility of establishing the setting and the characters in the first long shot. By the nature of the medium, only rarely does the camera try exactly to assume the vision of a central character, as in Robert Montgomery's *The Lady in the Lake.* More frequently the camera moves with the protagonists, but observes them, so that the function is more analogous to a third person narrator.

The African Queen opens with panoramic views of the jungle. The camera moves into the settlement from on high, suggesting immediately the conflict between the savage and the civilized parts of man's dual nature. The sound itself, jungle noises cacophonous and frightening, are modulated somewhat as we move, with the camera, down to the small chapel where the natives are singing a hymn—their own voices still echoing the sounds of the jungle, their singing so barbaric as to suggest strongly that they are only slightly removed from the raw jungle milieu themselves.

Henry V

Henry V never quite abandons the stylization which characterizes its opening long shot. We see a panoramic view of London, so still, so pregnant with cause, as to suggest Wordsworth's "On Westminster Bridge." But the town is still clearly a model, although an ingenious one, and in the spirit of one who admires a clever model, we move in with the camera until we find the Globe Theatre. It is not until we have a much closer shot of the theatre, and a man raising the flag which announces curtain time, that we can suspend our disbelief, and, having accepted the convention of the stylized set, watch the opening of a stage performance of *Henry V*.

Inside the theatre the camera suddenly becomes more flex-

35

Already thrown into confusion by the arrows of the English archers, the French cavalry in *Henry V* form a spectacular background for the figure of King Harry as he rallies his tired and weakened forces to another charge.

ible, roving around the pit and the galleries, watching spectators and gallants gathering and finally settling back to watch the entrance of the Chorus and listen to his first speech, in itself an account of the manner in which the imagination can transcend the wooden "O" and supply the actuality and richness of scene which the words suggest. "Piece out our imperfections with your thoughts," he says, and shortly thereafter the set before us becomes no longer a theatre; no longer are we watching a *performance* of a play as it might have been given in

Shakespeare's time, but we are in fact and mind transported just as the Chorus says, "Unto Southampton do we shift our scene," and watch the King embarking for France. Only at this point does the camera assume its full range of flexibility so that we may see King Harry's face glance up at the rigging or over at the elaborate preparations for the voyage.

Although we may move with Harry during the long watch before dawn and the critical battle at Agincourt, and even eavesdrop on his long soliloquy about the responsibility of leadership, we are always as removed from the action and inner thoughts as a spectator would be. Like a reporter, albeit a highly mobile one, we watch the preparations for battle in each camp and then the massing for the attack on the part of the French, and the grouping for defense, on the part of the English. We switch back and forth more and more rapidly, from the French cavalry, cumbersome, ornate, and arrogant, to the English archers, who, kneeling, draw their bows tighter and even tighter in anticipation until the final climactic release.

With the camera, the viewer never quite abandons the role of spectator to some giant pageant; this is as much the result of the point of view established in *Henry V* as it is of the settings, which even in the most realistic scenes utilize a background which is clearly a painted drop.

ATTITUDE

Whereas the location of the camera may mean simply its distance in space from the object it regards and hence establishes point of view in Henry James's sense, the angle from which the camera—and hence, the spectator—regards things may often instantly reveal the attitude of the director towards his subject and how he expects us to feel. This secondary implication of the term "point of view" is intricately related to the first and much more complex. Consider the multiple function of the camera in Orson Welles' *Citizen Kane,* a picture which will be analyzed in great detail in Chapter VI. One of its functions is to serve as the dispassionate observer, much as a newsreel camera would, whose purpose ostensibly is only to record what happens. For certain segments of the film, it does just that—especially when upon the event of his death it purports to give a summary of Citizen Kane's life. At other times, it assumes the attitudes and points of view of the various people who theoretically should have known Kane best, as each is interviewed in turn by the reporter eager to find out the riddle of Kane's last word, "Rosebud."

In turn, the camera assumed the knowledge which each person has of Kane. The effort to solve the riddle of "Rosebud" turns up piece after piece of a gigantic puzzle, fragments of a man's life, the whole of which is an enigma. So it is that the images, not only shots but whole sequences, are presented to us as fragments of a puzzle—beginning with the gate, then the vast and disorganized clutter of artifacts from all over the world, including the various accounts of his life from those close to him, and ending with an examination of his castle, after death, with his possessions—disorganized, pitiful, meaningless—scattered about, some never uncrated, awaiting cataloguing.

Between those sequences which look at Kane from particular points of view, those of his friends and employees, the camera moves with the inquiring eye of the reporter who is trying to put the pieces together and occasionally assumes a prerogative not normally allocated to the observer. At one point the camera moves through the air, down to a skylight, and through, with a kind of X-ray vision, to fix on Susan Kane as she sits forlornly at a table in her nightclub. Only toward the end when it travels freely through the bric-a-brac in Xanadu, does it reveal the secret to us—the secret which will never be known to the reporter, the trust officer, the business manager, the friend, the wife, or the avaricious steward. To some it may seem as if the giveaway by the camera is a violation of point of view; perhaps the real significance is contained in the sign which appears in the opening and closing shots: "No Trespassing." It seems to say that the dead are inviolate; no one dares intrude on this man's tragedy.

A further refinement appears in Kurosawa's *Rashomon,* which won the Grand Prize at the Venice Film Festival in 1951. Here the camera examines four principals in turn, each of whom gives an account of a murder and rape. As each principal gives his version of the episode, the camera reconstructs the events according to his testimony. That no resolution is ever made suggests strongly that the film is ultimately an inquiry into the nature of truth.[3]

The attitude of the beholder—and hence, of the director —is often revealed instantly by the angle from which he regards things. After Kane has lost the election, he and his friend Leland stand amidst the campaign rubbish in the deserted newspaper office. The camera is placed low, almost at shoe level; the defeated Kane, friend of the working man, defender of democratic principles, looms high, oddly distorted, ironically larger than life.

The camera makes another comment as it views Kane after he has married the girl whom he tried to make a singer. Dwarfed by the pointless monstrosity of the castle, Kane stands far from us in the fireplace, engulfed by its opening, a tiny and forlorn figure, no longer capable of love. Far away from him, actually and symbolically, all communication destroyed, sits his wife—working on a puzzle.

The Russian film, *A Summer to Remember,* is weakened by its ideological portrayal of the Russian communes. When it deals only with the vision of the little boy from whose point of view the story is told, it is moving and true. The boy awaits the arrival of his new stepfather, apprehensively enough. The camera is at floor level, physically and emotionally on a plane

[3] See Arthur Knight's account in *The Liveliest Art* (New York, Macmillan, 1957), pp. 248-249.

with the boy and the toy soldiers with which he is playing. We see across the toys to the entrance of the stepfather, watching his boots enter and halt. The arrival causes the boy to upset his pieces, and the game is literally disrupted, as the world of the child has been disrupted by the strange adult.

In addition, we tend to associate certain emotions and attitudes with the quality of vision as registered by the camera. Soft outlines and blurred distances suggest nostalgia, affection, despair; hard outlines and sharp contrasts, fear, apprehension, anger; distortion, by whatever technical method, suggests intoxication, panic, insanity. The whirling world of William Wyler's *The Lost Weekend* is seen as though we ourselves were suffering from delirium tremens. Images blur, fade, dissolve, and resolve into hideous and grotesque caricatures in *The Snake Pit*. The chase up the Eiffel Tower in Charles Crichton's *The Lavender Hill Mob* subjects the viewers to a disquieting vertigo as the camera whirls around and around.

MEANING

"In the film all visible things act." [4] By calling our attention to them, the camera forces all objects, as well as all people, to make some contribution to the total meaning of the film. The movement of the camera, the location of the camera, and the angle from which the shot is taken are all means of concentrating on an effect which the director wishes to produce. But the work of the director also includes the cutting or editing of the sequences he has on film; such editing is responsible for the final form of the movie and a very large part of its meaning. The final arrangement is the result of all the techniques at the editor's disposal, including juxtaposing for contrast, tension, or ironic effect; of placing shots in sequence to show simultaneity; of repeating to underscore or emphasize,

[4] Georg Schmidt, Werner Schmalenbach, and Peter Bächlin, *The Film* (London, Falcon, 1948), p. 22.

to suggest similarity, and hence to enlarge meaning through the perception of resemblance among disparate things.

Editing means simply the judicious cutting apart and rejoining in a more significant order of the film after it has been processed. The camera may shift suddenly from one object to another, from the face of a startled girl, staring open-mouthed at a fresh corpse, to an onrushing locomotive, whose shrill whistle blast is metaphorically the scream we never heard. We may watch one scene gradually give way to another so that the first lingers, superimposed on the second, until it fades. Rapid cutting back and forth and perhaps shortening the time allotted to each sequence, may result in the tension developed in the description of the battle of Agincourt. The sequence of village ladies gossiping (in song) in Morton da Costa's filmed version of *The Music Man* gives way to an overhead view of their hats, flounced and feathered, making the suggestion of their biddylike quality explicit. (As if afraid we will miss this visual metaphor, the director cuts to a yard where real hens are picking and clucking.)

Such editing, then, is the principal device available to the director with which to order his shots. As we will show in more detail in subsequent chapters, he can organize the action into significant patterns; he may create, sustain, and modulate the rhythm of sequences; he may manipulate time to serve his own purposes, interrupting the flow, moving backward through time, then ahead again, in order to produce the most effective and dynamic arrangements possible.

Tone, as well as meaning, may be established by the director's use of color, which is of course capable of profoundly affecting the emotions, as well as carrying certain traditionally associated meanings. It would seem that color photography might enhance a picture which is primarily realistic. Yet not all stories profit from its use. As if to support the argument that film is an art form in itself and therefore cannot really render us "a slice of life," certain films demand black and white treatment rather than color. Whereas the use of color may heighten the effect of a melodramatic or romantic story, Kurosawa's *Gate of Hell* relies on symbolic reds and blues throughout; Ingmar Bergman's *The Seventh Seal* needs the contrast of black and white as an intrinsic ingredient. It would be interesting to see what Bergman would do with color.

The Seventh Seal opens with a shot of the ocean, timeless, colorless, forever in flux. On a gray beach we find the knight and his squire, recently returned from the Crusades. The figure of death, ambiguously dressed like a monk, black cowl over white face, appears and challenges the knight to a chess match. The knight will remain alive until he has lost the game. Chess figures are black and white; black and white, death and life, evil and good are the counters of this film, and every shot is composed with such attention to chiaroscuro as to evoke constantly the eternal questions which have plagued man from the start. The sequence at the end is typical. The poor, ingenuous, and innocent entertainer, with his baby boy, and wife, watches as the figure of Death leads the other characters, knight, squire, knight's wife, and all, up a long slope, in silhouette, black against white, in the dance of death.

At times the use of color is self-evident and adds a depth of meaning. After making love to Tony, Maria, in *West Side Story,* who has earlier appeared in a white bridal dress, now appears in a red one. On certain rare occasions, color may make a direct and functional contribution, as it does in the fantasy *The Wizard of Oz*. The world of Kansas, ordinary and pedestrian, is photographed in monochrome. When Dorothy is swept up by the tornado and deposited in Oz, the transformation into this fairyland is heralded by a blaze of color, in the yellow brick road, in the flowers in the Emerald City.

The combination of the flexibility of the camera, the editing in the cutting room, and a host of special effects enables the film to create its own temporal and spatial world, with its special associations the direct result of the conscious stream. It can create a world that never was nor ever could be, a world where the laws which prevail in our own reality are suspended and ordinary relationships among objects abolished. Thus it is that the techniques of the moving picture are peculiarly suited to exploitation by the teller of fairy tales and the surrealist. They can create their own fantastic worlds governed only by their imagination and the special laws which operate within them. Jean Cocteau, for instance, can reconstruct a fairy tale like *Beauty and the Beast,* building for our own experience a castle where invisible servants produce food and drink, and candelabra supported by human arms sprout from the walls to light the heroine down the corridors. We accept without questioning the metamorphosis of the Beast into the Prince just as we did when we were children and such a world was more probable.

In a world of this kind, all natural laws as we know them are susceptible to suspension. Inanimate objects are endowed with life. Visual aspects of the world are transformed and distorted. Solid bodies become transparent. The ghost of Hamlet's father appears, doomed for a certain time to walk, not this earth, but the battlements of Elsinore in Olivier's *Hamlet.*

The animated cartoon, a special development in itself, represents perhaps the purest demonstration of cinematic possibilities, once we have accepted the convention of the drawing and the ensuing world of the artist. The comic strip itself illustrates many of the techniques available to the director in terms of emphasis, selection, omission, distortion, point of view, and tone. The animated cartoon, in color or black and white, is but an extremely sophisticated development of the comic strip —a marriage of comic strip and moving picture techniques. Certain cartoon characters, like Donald Duck and Mickey Mouse, or the Seven Dwarfs or Mr. Magoo, are as true creations in their way as Ahab, Oliver Twist, and Tom Sawyer and have an existence in the country of the mind with other

Up the eerie battlements of Elsinore goes Hamlet, to challenge his father's ghost. The midnight hour and the supernatural appearance are both enlightened by the fog and the blurred outlines of the set.

immortals. In watching such pictures we are consciously making concessions to the form, respecting its conventions and acknowledging the world they present as fictitiously real. Nowhere are the particular conventions more conspicuous than when they are flouted, as in the unfortunate introduction of photographed human beings among cartoon characters in several Disney films—*Saludos Amigos,* for example.

Exclusive of the animated cartoon, all the technical developments of the moving picture art, including increasing flexibility of the camera, special lenses, film, and inspired editing, culminate in certain so-called avant-garde films whose impact on American audiences has been considerable and whose reception has been marked by violent extremes of praise and censure. As the director has assumed greater and greater control over the picture, as opposed to the earlier corporate efforts of large companies, and as his eye and his imagination have become surer, the result has been films which are extensive in vision, as far as cinematography goes, and intensive in perception—being more and more concerned with the psychological

44

life of the individual and less and less with overt action for its own sake. The analogy of such films as Antonioni's *L'Avventura* and Resnais' *Last Year at Marienbad* with the novels of James Joyce is inescapable. The series of images flashing on the screen is ordered not by space and time as we commonly know them but a space and time created by the mind. The audience for such films is often troubled, frequently vexed by what it finds makes demands on creative and perceptive powers far beyond the usual Hollywood product. The audience for Woolf or Joyce is similarly limited and must be trained. This does not mean that Joyce and Woolf are not significant writers, nor that the films cited are aberrations.

Consciousness of art does not nullify the experience of art. The spectator who immerses himself in the stream of art, who surrenders his critical faculties completely while he is suspended vicariously in the experience, is paradoxically at a disadvantage, for he will be unable not only to evaluate the experience but will indeed be prevented from the highest kind of fulfillment. Unless he understands what he has seen, he will not even have seen what there is to see. The moviegoer is at a special kind of disadvantage, for most of us see a movie only once. But by critical examination of a few movies, the spectator will become a more thorough participant in other movies. He will ask not only, "What shot will come next?" but "Why?" He will become sensitive to the effect of certain assumptions by the camera, to the use of contrast and repetition, to the juxtaposition of shots, to the use of color, or of composition in black and white, and to the accretion of meaning by objects in the film as a result of the deliberate attention devoted to them.

CHAPTER FOUR

The Lively Art

THE CONVENTIONS OF MOVIE MAKING

Suppose a director were planning to shoot one scene from Lillian Smith's novel, *Strange Fruit*. Doctor Sam Perry, a Negro, is waiting to see Tom Harris, owner of a large mill. He is hoping that Tom can forestall an impending lynching. As he waits, both impatiently and fearfully, Sam is thinking: "Ten minutes to six. Soon be knocking off time. Soon be two hundred more to swell the restlessness downtown."

The director must now make a complex set of decisions. Should he shoot the scene from Sam's point of view? Should it be more direct, narrative? "Ten minutes to six." A shot of the clock may take care of establishing the time. How establish the near immediacy of "knocking off time"? Should it be done with dialogue? Should the idea be planted in the preceding sequence? What should be done about the mill workers as six o'clock approaches? Should there be a sequence of shots of particular characters in particular stances—one readying a noose, another grinning evilly, yet another honing a wicked knife? Or do these details sound like film clichés? How shall the "influx of two hundred more" be communicated? Should the camera look down upon the mill interior in a long shot? And meanwhile, can the "restlessness" downtown be conveyed visually? If so, how? Shall invented details, not from the novel, be used? Would a rapid juxtaposition of preparations downtown and readiness at the mill enhance the growing tension? Meanwhile, shots of Sam—staring at the clock, sweat beading his forehead, fingers clenching and unclenching—can be inter-cut into the other sequences. How often shall the camera look at the clock? At 5:55, or 5:58? Or both? Should the clock shots be taken from the same angle each time? Would a close-up be more effective?

What about background sounds? Should there be a rising intensity in musical accompaniment? Stark silence? Any dia-logue? Which mill sounds might be exploited?

If the film shots are sequential and of the same length, one effect is created. If each sequence is shorter in number of frames than the one preceding it, the effect is a speeding up and a heightening of tension.

For the film maker, control of the camera means control of the point of view, the *how* a viewer perceives reality. A close-up is not only a more intimate, probing view, it enlarges awareness and points up the unseen or unnoticed. It serves to eliminate what the director decides is less important. It inten-sifies whatever it focuses upon. The close-up may give signifi-cance to inanimate objects. It permits significant details or parts to stand for symbolically larger wholes. It is a visual underlining, a visual exclamation mark, a rendering of experi-ence in spatial terms.

Among the familiar shots in the film lexicon is the con-ventional focusing on a drawer containing a hidden pistol, a cross symbolically observed, a head slumping to one side sig-nifying death. Contrast these standard film clichés with the scuttling rats in a long-empty swimming pool in *Sunset Boule-vard,* symbolizing the decay of a former opulence. As freshness of verbal imagery delights the reader of poetry, so freshness of visual images delights the viewer of moving pictures.

A novelist may deliberately choose language that pro-duces ambiguity and complexity. However, film symbols tend toward the real, the concrete. They tend to be less ambiguous. Some film directors like Alain Resnais and Jean Renoir have deliberately conveyed a richness of meaning through complex pictorial images. For example, in *Last Year at Marienbad,* Resnais cares less about telling a story than about evoking complex emotional responses. The picture raises questions about time, point of view, values, and meaning. While the film's verbal statements are repeated—or modified slightly— the emotional power depends less upon verbal statements than on visual symbols, symbols free of a simple one-to-one meaning. Resnais uses formal gardens, a baroque castle, a mathematical matchstick game, a pistol range, a statue, a crumbled wall, unusual angles, long staircases and corridors, and a variety of distance shots and contexts for such shots to create ambiguity and tension. Even verbal statements or pictorial statements take on changing coloration as their film contexts vary. The film produces a range of moods—sometimes existentialist, sometimes decadent, sometimes passionate. The audience leaves the theatre debating alternative interpretations. Nor can any critical observation explain all the nuances of tone and feeling. Like a complex novel, the ambiguities enhance the richness and pictorial splendor of the picture. It is significant to note that the film's function was not narration but evocation of mood, feeling, and philosophy.

While a film like *Last Year at Marienbad* concentrates on the mental states and emotions of its characters—hovering over them in Joycean fashion—most films concentrate upon narrative. The novelist using verbal symbols has several advantages over such conventional films. He may transcend his story line and engage in philosophic speculation, in introspective study of his characters, and in discursive probing of characterization. He may suggest social or political implications stemming from his narrative and do so quickly and economically in space. Pictures, however, are frozen in space. They tend away from the abstract to the concrete. Yet it is abstract language that enlarges upon narrative and description. When Joseph Conrad wrote, "My task which I am trying to achieve is, by the power of the written word, to make you hear, to make you feel—it is, before all, to make you *'see'*," he intended not only a physical seeing but a mental apperception.[1] The novel, particularly the modern novel, has tended to move from external action to internal thought and speculation. It has shifted from an emphasis on plot to a probing of character. Even sociological themes have made for psychological insights. The novel moves toward a density and complexity that would be impractical for film to emulate. Thus, critics who belabor motion pictures adapted from novels miss the verbal elements that evaporate in the cinematic treatment. But their assumptions move toward equating the media. Literature's verbal power cannot be superimposed upon a visual medium. And films made from literary sources *must* shift to cinematic values if they are to maintain artistic integrity. These include a sense of realism, emotional immediacy, the sweep of seething excitement, the power of shots and sequences to evoke response, and the editing which stabilizes film details in aesthetic patterns.

NOVEL INTO FILM

As the moving picture evolved, the search for stories led to literary sources. Films adapted from novels consistently ranked high among the industry's productions and vied for its Academy Awards. Commercially successful films like *Lost Horizon, David Copperfield, Gone with the Wind, From Here to Eternity,* and *Quo Vadis* enhanced the reputation of the novel as a valuable motion picture property. Prestigious novels, including Pulitzer Prize winners like *The Good Earth, All the King's Men, The Grapes of Wrath, A Bell for Adano,* and *The Bridge of San Luis Rey,* made successful motion pictures.

The movies had a secondary impact on the readers of novels. As library circulation statistics and book sales figures

---

[1] Joseph Conrad, Preface to *The Nigger of the Narcissus,* in Frank W. Cushwa, *An Introduction to Conrad* (New York, Odyssey, 1933), p. 225.

reveal in study after study, popular films produce a mass public eager to read the novels from which the films were made. Jerry Wald has pointed out that Hollywood's production of *Lost Horizon* spurred sales of the book to an incredible 1,400,000.

Curiously enough, the American moving picture industry has often manifested a reluctance to write its own movies. Like the television industry and other mass media, it has been subject to prevailing commercial impulses. With the exception of the western and the horror picture, the industry has preferred to pay an inordinate price—sometimes hundreds of thousands of dollars—for a play or a book that has already proved successful, rather than engage a writer to write an original script. At times, Hollywood has not been above buying an expensive (though otherwise mediocre or tasteless) property and plugging it until it has attained respectable sales, before making a movie. In such cases when they have bought a property, they are perfectly willing to engage a recognized author to write the script, working from the novel or play. But in the past such an author has been low man in the caste system, and some, like Nathanael West, Scott Fitzgerald, and others, have been shattered or destroyed or have left Hollywood.

In the making of motion pictures from fiction or drama, fidelity of detailed reproduction became a touchstone by which to measure motion pictures. One common assumption appeared in such critical commentary. Observers tended to equate the media. They assumed a detachable content in literary works that could be reinstated visually. They further assumed that dialogue could supplement such details as were not primarily visual. They failed to recognize the inherent and significant differences among the media. Each has its own conventions, its own style.

The novelist can cover a great deal of time quickly in a simple statement denoting the passage of time. When a character in fiction gets older, the writer merely notes the number of years that have passed. Again, the film is less flexible and must solve this problem cinematically. In *Great Expectations,* Pip becomes older in a dramatic visual sequence. We see the younger Pip in his blacksmith's garb, and then we see him, through a dissolve, several years later dressed in the height of fashion as he prepares for his "great expectations." The camera focuses first at his feet and then pans upward until we see Pip, the young gentleman. The passage of time is also conveyed economically by a montage of shots as Pip acquires the gentleman's veneer. We watch him getting instruction in dancing, boxing, fencing—the montage is comparable to the training of Eliza Doolittle in *Pygmalion.*

Unique to the film medium is the dissolve, wherein one picture becomes stronger and replaces the earlier shot. This transitional device also serves as a means both for linking symbols and for deliberately juxtaposing particulars for specific effects. Also unique to the film are superimposed shots; words must appear in linear and consecutive sequence; hence there is no verbal equivalent for the double exposure. These film devices enhance the quality of immediacy which is unique to the film medium.

When the Joads start cross country in John Ford's *The Grapes of Wrath,* we follow much of their journey with glimpses of road signs, names of towns, states, rivers. In a few moments Ford symbolizes the vastness of distance, the unending journey. An overloaded truck silhouetted against the sky, a sign saying "camp 50¢" and another sign saying "water 15¢ a gallon," all these indicate the desperate conditions of the Okies, as well as man's inhumanity to man. The indomitable progress of the Joads is shown by a series of signs reading "Leaving New Mexico," "Arizona Welcomes You," and "Colorado River." The sign "Needles Welcomes You to California" contrasts ironically with the forbidding scenery.

In *The Grapes of Wrath,* both flashbacks and dissolves are employed. At the beginning of the film when Tom and Muley meet at the deserted family farm, Muley is explaining what happened while Tom was in prison. The camera creeps up close to Muley.

He says ". . . a man come one day," and the film dissolves to the scene Muley has been describing. Moments later, the camera turns to Muley, and he continues, "They come with the cats . . ."; and a dissolve (and flashback) reveal the day when the "cat" knocked down Muley's house, followed by another dissolve to the present, where Muley, looking half-demented, shows signs of the torment inflicted by the past. Thus, technical devices link past and present. Later in the same film, a dissolve is used to suggest an ironic relationship. When the Okies are offered work by a labor recruiter in a car, the film dissolves to the work area—an area jammed with police and with workers unwilling to be exploited. The Joads recognize that they are strikebreakers, but hunger and fear corrode men's scruples. Thus, the hope promised by the labor recruiter suddenly has dissolved into an unpleasant game in which the Joads are pawns.

When Ma Joad disposes of her mementoes before the family begins its cross country trip, the camera comes up close; we see her throwing away a postcard of the Statue of Liberty. There is no verbal comment; the audience can perceive the contrast between the Statue of Liberty symbol and the state of the Joads, driven from their home. At the close of the film, a short shot precedes the long shot. In the reversal, Ma says, "We're the people . . . ," implying their undying, indestructible spirit. Then the camera dissolves to more trucks, more people moving along the road, to the large "we" of the novel.

In *The Bridge of San Luis Rey,* juxtaposition of shots creates a scene of horror. Brother Juniper, the narrator, wonders why the bridge fell and what meaning the event holds. The camera flashes back to the first weakening and pulling of the bridge's fibers; then it shifts to the people crossing the bridge; once more the camera returns to the further tearing of the bridge's supports. And once more the camera shifts toward the people on, crossing, or safely over the bridge. We see the rapid deterioration counterpointed against the people unknowingly flirting with fate; the quick shots leave us uncertain about the victims' identities. Furthermore, this scene comes near the end of the film after the audience has developed a sympathy for some of the characters. Thus the alternating shots convey not only a sense of immediate terror but a growing sense of fear; who will be the victims and why they? The excitement and tension of the film flow from the technique used by the director in arranging the order of his shots.

PLAY INTO FILM

Stage performances utilize many of the same conventions as do moving pictures, for similar purposes. Both present sight and sound to a watching audience. Both are interested in relating stories. Both recreate worlds; both use actors, props, and sets to produce desired effects. In each, movement is essential. Each uses the present tense, primarily, although the flashback is available to it. Finally, both are presented to an audience gathered together in a darkened theatre, an audience that has paid an admission fee and waits with certain expectations.

Yet because the film is primarily visual, it depends largely upon those conventions which affect the eye—imaginative shooting and editing of shots, and sequences intelligently joined. If the film content is thematic, appropriate images and symbols must be sought to produce the desired effect.

The stage performance, stagebound and less flexible, is primarily a verbal medium depending on a richness of language, augmented by expression and movement, to carry its freight of meaning. Film, free from the confining physical limits of time and space, ranges quickly across distances and can suspend time or withdraw into the back reaches of earlier time periods. In its rapid sequence of realistic, alternating shots, the motion picture can leave one setting, return shortly, and leave again—depending on the director's purposes. The juxtaposing of pictures heightens the sense of immediacy.

The movies have a far richer external, physical world available for exploration than the staged performance. The stage cannot show us, in anything like the same way, mountains, streams, forests, skies; no matter how skillful the construction, on stage we are aware of the artificiality; such exciting and panoramic images must be invoked in the mind. If the stage performance wishes to show the forces of nature—tornadoes, typhoons, blizzards, dust storms—it must depend largely upon verbal descriptions and reports of off-stage events. Therefore, plays concentrate, not on physical phenomena, but on intense human relationships and complexities. Film as a medium can cope with spectacles, crowd scenes, street scenes of bustling excitement, panoramic visual scenes of beauty, grandeur, and scope.

The dramatic play permits—and even encourages—greater introspection and philosophic inquiry than the film form. Since films are primarily visual, verbal elements tend to be less important than in a play. The most direct sensory appeal in motion pictures is to the eye, not the ear, although musical effects often anticipate and lead the way to action. The theatre permits more complex human relationships, more complex states of mind. In the motion picture the least successful scenes are those in which visual meanings are subordinated to extensive talk. Hence Shakespeare's plays are difficult to transfer to film. During the "To be or not to be" soliloquy in Olivier's *Hamlet,* the camera tries desperately to accompany the speech; the camera creeps in close to peer at Hamlet; it focuses on the churning seas and the austere castle; it examines Hamlet's mannerisms and gestures. Sometimes close-ups reveal Hamlet voicing the words; other times the words come out of the sound track as if he were thinking them. But the scene remains static.

The evocative words, the complex play of ideas and images, these demand attention, distract the viewer from the inquisitive camera, and compete with the visual picture. Probably the most common criticism of film is its "unfaithfulness" to the play's verbal elements—the play's conceptualizing, its complexity of characterization, its philosophic speculation, its language. In the Spring issue of the 1945 *Kenyon Review,* Eric Bentley observed: "The potentialities of the talking screen differ from those of the silent screen in adding the dimension of dialogue—which could be poetry." In "Style and Medium in the Motion Pictures" in *Critique,* on the other hand, Erwin Panofsky said: "The potentialities of the talking screen differ from those of the silent screen in integrating visible movement with dialogue, which, therefore, had better not be poetry." [2] And William Gibson, whose play, *The Miracle Worker,* began as a television performance, became a successful Broadway hit drama, and has since received a deserved critical acclaim as a fine film, wrote: "The camera is the most facile medium in the world to write for; with the free run of time and place it can untie one story knot at a time and skip on, and has such transparency as a medium that it not only does not need, but is burdened by, too many words. . . ." [3]

As in any play by Shakespeare, the language in *Hamlet* poses problems for an adapter. When the Ghost speaks to Hamlet and says,

> I could a tale unfold whose lightest word
> Would harrow up thy soul, freeze thy young
>   blood,
> Make thy two eyes like stars start from
>   their spheres,
> Thy knotted and combined locks to part,
> And each particular hair to stand on end,
> Like quills upon the fretful porpentine.

[2] Erwin Panofsky, "Style and Medium in Motion Pictures," *Critique,* 1:3 (January-February, 1947), 9.

[3] William Gibson, *Dinny and the Witches, The Miracle Worker, Two Plays by William Gibson* (New York, Atheneum, 1960), p. 14.

the motion picture director is faced with several difficult alternatives. He can point his camera at the Ghost, at Hamlet, at both—and let the evocative words be spoken. If he does, there is a pull in two directions—the visual on the screen against the power of the words to produce imaginative horrors on the screen of the mind. Another alternative might be to eliminate the dialogue, since the plot requires only the line, "Revenge his foul and most unnatural murder." The truth is that no filmed or staged "horrors" can match Shakespeare's rich evocative language.

As the Ghost continues speaking, he describes, in specific detail, his sleeping in the orchard when his brother poured poison into his ear. In the play within a play, the same details are repeated. Olivier films a sequence showing the actual murder scene. In this instance he enlarges upon a reference which is verbally rich but static film potential and turns it to visual capital.

In adapting a play to a motion picture, the writer may enlarge its scope. Dialogue is frequently edited and curtailed, while details are actually enlarged. A single stage scene requires many shots and sequences. Visual particulars must replace verbal references. In *Abe Lincoln in Illinois,* the play refers to, but does not show, the death of Ann Rutledge. In the film, however, two actual scenes replace the reference to her death. At a political dance celebrating Abe's candidacy for the Assembly, Ann collapses. In the next sequence of shots, Lincoln delivers a political speech. The subsequent sequence takes us out to Ann's cottage and the scene of her death. Visual particularity replaces verbal reference.

One further series of sequences in the film underlines the kinds of changes made in translation from drama to motion picture. The play opens after Abraham Lincoln has established himself in New Salem. In the film, with its greater scope, a conventional long shot shows us a log cabin with the year 1831 superimposed upon it. A closer shot focuses on the window of the cabin with Abe's father staring out into the rain. The point of view now shifts; the next sequences are indoor shots as the camera follows Tom Lincoln until he turns away from the rain. The camera then pans to Abe reading a book before the fire. When his father observes, "It's raining but you wouldn't notice, your nose everlastin' stuck in some book," the tone of the film has been established, more by visual selections than verbal clues.

While the film *Abe Lincoln in Illinois* exploits initial sequences prepared for the movie and not in the original play, the film *The Crucible* concludes with a number of sequences not in the play but hinted at in the dramatic content. As the final curtain rings down on the play, John Proctor is being marched to his death. The sound effects are symbolic of the offstage hanging. The stage direction reads: "The final drumroll crashes, then heightens violently. . . ." The audience does not see the details. In the film the victims to be hanged are readied; the camera pans down so we see only their legs and watch the supports pushed out beneath them. Following the deaths, the crowd surges in and the victims are carried off—almost like heroic victors; perhaps with their lives they have broken the excesses of tyranny in Puritan Massachusetts. The spirit of the film is faithful to the spirit of the play, but the details reduce the level of abstraction and add visually powerful particulars.

Film directors, like stage directors, frequently invent attractive "business" to embellish existing scenes. For film, such details must be cinematically sound. In Sir Laurence Olivier's *Hamlet,* we see Polonius giving fatherly advice to Laertes, who maintains a serious decorum through the ordeal despite his eagerness to get away. While Polonius delivers his sonorous clichés, the camera catches Ophelia tickling her brother, putting her arms around him, tapping him mischievously on the back. The pompous speech is cleverly undercut by visual details. As Holden Caulfield observes in *The Catcher in the Rye,* Ophelia is ". . . horsing around with her brother, taking his dagger out of the holster, and teasing him and all while he was trying to look interested in the bull his father was shooting." Holden then adds, "I get a big bang out of that. But you don't see that kind of stuff much." The criticism is valid; it takes imaginative direction to add the purely cinematic details requisite to motion picture art. As Rudolf Arnheim notes, too many film directors fail to ". . . make much original use of the artistic means at their disposal. They do not produce works of art but tell the people stories."

In Arthur Penn's *The Miracle Worker,* Annie Sullivan has been disciplining Helen Keller. A fretful father asks Miss Sullivan, "Do you love her?" intending to rebuke her for cruelty. But Annie Sullivan knows her excellent reasons for administering discipline; she also knows that parents who love their children nevertheless sometimes take the easiest way out. She hesitates only a moment and then replies, "Do you?" The camera focuses on Captain Keller's face. His is the sin of omission; both know it. Annie has cut to the quick; he is honest enough to know it. All this is in his face; no words are needed. When Annie tries to instill a sense of responsibility into the spoiled child, a violent physical battle ensues between them. This scene occupies six pages of description in the stage directions of the play; it takes up an even greater section of the film and is utterly exhausting to the audience. It uses no dialogue, yet it establishes the struggle between two willful and capable individuals. It is a most compelling scene in a film already powerful, and it does not use words.

In *The Miracle Worker,* we frequently watch a present scene becoming more faint on screen, while a contrasting scene from the past becomes dominant in Annie Sullivan's consciousness. At strategic moments she remembers her brother Jimmy. In one series of shots, we watch Annie's face when the statement is made, "Dinner will be ready right away." Slowly the film scene dissolves as Annie recalls the violence of youngsters fighting; superimposed (co-existing) is a shot of Helen Keller's

Deaf child and determined tutor struggle in *The Miracle Worker.*

frantic reaching. The deliberately grainy quality of the film suggests the persistence of memory. We, the audience, perceive the relationships and early experiences making Annie Sullivan what she is. No verbal clues are necessary.

The peculiar ability of the camera to focus our attention on objects and hence instill meaning into them is particularly evident in this movie, which is itself concerned with the difficulty of communication. Annie Sullivan has been trying to teach words to her blind and deaf student. She has been spelling words into the blind girl's hand, word after word after word, knowing that the deaf need to begin with a concept of the relationship of language to things and ideas. Annie knows

59

that once the concept of language is grasped, a torrent of progress will follow, including understanding of human relationships and communication. In a series of shots we see water in a basin, water in the form of rain, water in a running stream, water in a glass. Each time, the word *water* is given to Helen. Finally, as Annie pumps water and Helen puts her hands under the gushing stream, she puts together the word and the actual thing the language refers to. This affecting moment has been prepared for in scene after scene. The first word of speech, a babyish rendering of the word water, brings with it a powerful emotional reaction. The key to language, to Helen Keller's understanding, to her eventual speaking, has been found.

RESOURCES OF THE CAMERA

The flexibility of the movie camera combined with technical facility gives the motion picture director much greater versatility than the stage director. The camera angle permits him to add to the theatrical limitation of seeing straight ahead. Shooting upward produces quite different effects from shooting downward. Fading in and out permits the stage equivalent of a slow curtain or long blackout without calling it to one's attention forcefully, as would happen with excessive curtain closings. The dissolve forcefully links juxtaposed images for particular effects, while superimposed images permit instantaneous cause and effect relationships to be symbolized. It also allows for similarities to be exploited. In an early Charlie Chaplin film, *The Gold Rush,* Charlie, starving to death, cooks his old boots like a roast for supper, eats them deliberately and gracefully, stowing the nails like bones on the side of his dish and eating the laces like spaghetti. When an equally hungry villain sees Charlie, the power of a dissolve turns him into a chicken trussed for roasting. In *The Miracle Worker,* Annie Sullivan remembers her brother, James, as she ponders how to help

Helen Keller. The superimposed shots give us past, present, and their relationship—and help us to understand Annie Sullivan more completely even as we observe her in the present.

Judicious juxtaposition of shots, for the purposes of contrast or emphasis, heightens visual communication. In *The Day of the Painter,* a spoof of action painting, all dialogue has been eliminated. In one sense, human behavior is commented upon through the actions of ducks placidly observing the painter. The quizzical and slightly incredulous seeming expressions natural to ducks are used by the film's director to comment on the artist's behavior.

Clever juxtaposition of sequences may produce lovely comic effects. In *Modern Times,* Chaplin's opening shot pictures rushing sheep; the following sequence shows rushing workingmen. The parallel shots make their point, visually. In a silent film, *The Immigrant,* a boat is seen rolling horribly and we get a picture of seasick passengers; at this point we see Charlie Chaplin, back to the camera, hanging over the side of the boat—legs kicking, head down. Our expectations leap ahead of our knowledge. But the next sequence shows Charlie as he pulls himself up, eyes gleaming in triumph. He has hooked a large fish with his walking stick. In *Monsieur Verdoux,* a contrasting long shot and close-up serve a function similar to the juxtaposed shots. The long shot reveals a lovely lake, boat, attractive skies, and water—an idyllic picture. A close-up follows, and we see Monsieur Verdoux. He is about to murder another victim.

Powerful cinematic close-ups, soul searching or symbolic, add another technical dimension to film art. The camera can focus on details that would otherwise go unnoticed; it adds the power of a fresh viewpoint even when applied to familiar faces or objects. The stage play is like a series of long shots. In a play significant meaning can be attached to inanimate objects only when the director has called attention to the objects. The director of a motion picture has greater flexibility with his camera. The close-up not only focuses intensely but also serves to eliminate whatever the director does not wish to show.

The greater flexibility of film over stage plays usually means enlarging the scope of the play and increasing not only the number of characters and scenes but adding a wide variety of technical shots—the close-up, the angle shots, and framed visual shots. The spectrum of technical film devices that have become standard reveals the tremendous virtuosity and flexibility of film conventions.

Silent movies developed many communicative devices that were exclusively visual. For example, the chase sequences using speeded up action produced hilarious comic impact. A rapid alternation of shots in melodramatic situations became popular and effective. The camera would alternate rapidly between the heroine in some ghastly danger and the hero, or infantry, or what-have-you, rushing to the rescue. These Griffith chases, as they became known in honor of D. W. Griffith, a great innovator, can still be seen in variations today. We have our cowboy and Indian sequences, our cops and robbers, our action thrillers of all kinds. The alternation of shots, or crosscutting as it is technically known, heightens the tension and increases involvement.

In the silent screen days directors tended to improvise their daily shooting, rarely using a prepared script. They combined the realism inherent in film with a fantasy that was willingly believed by audiences—a 20th century suspension of disbelief, what Disney calls, "The possible impossible." Thus another convention was established. The audience knew that Harold Lloyd would get thumped by the careening automobile but remain essentially unhurt. He would teeter on the edge of a perilously high roof but remain unharmed. Gross clues could alert the audience to forthcoming slapstick violence, while they remained safe in the further knowledge that the movies might titillate and involve them but that Harold would ultimately succeed. Modern slapstick follows similar patterns; when Jerry Lewis or Bob Hope gets embroiled in a potentially lethal situation, the audience's awareness of a standard convention assures them that their suspension of reality will not be violated by the film maker. They can enjoy their temporary uneasiness.

During the period of pretalkies, the slapstick comic routines of Charlie Chaplin, Buster Keaton, Harold Lloyd, and the Mack Sennett Keystone Cops speeded up the film to produce some of the most hilarious chases in the history of mankind. The same chase persists in more serious and realistic fashion today in the western film, a basic film genre. In *The Wonderful World of Comedy,* an anthology of expertly edited scenes selected from Harold Lloyd's early comedies, the film is deliberately speeded up. Madcap automobiles and trolleys career through traffic; Harold Lloyd races through all sorts of danger—at better than Olympic speeds—to rescue the heroine. Perhaps the closest stage approach to the zany speeded up chase of helmeted cops, fetching flappers, and assorted characters occurred in the Broadway musical *On the Town* where trick lighting achieved similar effects, except, of course, for the unique film close-ups.

Both the freeze and the speedup lend themselves well to comedy. Masters in comedy like Charlie Chaplin, Ben Turpin, and Harold Lloyd used the technique. The speedup is the trademark of those hilarious chases marking early comedy and even modern comic chases such as the two unforgettable scenes in *The Lavender Hill Mob.* The speedup is also useful in establishing suspense and excitement. The audience willingly accepts the fantasy substituting for film's usual realism.

Panning is the process of rotating the camera to follow the action. The director can thus concentrate the attention of the viewer on those particulars he wishes to emphasize. Superimposed shots are what the term suggests—two pictures share the scene, suggesting both simultaneity and relationship, the film equivalent of a stream of consciousness. Superimposed shots in *The Miracle Worker* show that specific moments in the present are analogous to Annie Sullivan's memory of moments in the past. In *The Bridge of San Luis Rey,* Lynn Bari as the heroine receives instruction in acting. Her mentor calls out, "Anger," "Joy," and on screen we see shot fade into shot as she registers each emotion. Because the dissolves are very slow, they have almost the appearance of superimposed shots and suggest a heavy pressure on the learner by a demanding instructor.

An iris-in shot gives us a shot gradually enlarged, beginning as a small circle, finally encompassing the entire screen; this device allows the viewer to see an event and then the context which may comment upon or enlarge the meaning of the original smaller detail. In Harold Lloyd's *The Freshman,* for example, we see an iris shot of Harold, leading a football cheer. The iris continues to open to reveal the mirror against which he has been practicing. The iris-out is one kind of fade-out. The scene disappears as a contrasting circle of blackness blots out the screen.

In movies which show activity aboard submarines, we are sometimes allowed to see on the screen the picture which the captain is actually watching through his periscope. The result looks like what one sees through a pair of high-powered binoculars. Keyhole-shaped pictures, heart-shaped shots, circle-shaped shots are also used. The critical viewer asks only whether the technique is appropriate to the subject and not simply a gimmick. In *The Music Man,* we see a split screen and two separate pictures, side by side. The two simultaneous shots are essentially related to each other; in one, Marian, the heroine, sings a solo; in the other a quartet harmonizes. The shots are complementary.

Two other technical conventions are much used in film. The first is the fade-in or fade-out, equivalent to a slow curtain. The film fade has two major advantages: it allows for a smooth transition from scene to scene, and secondly, it may be used much more frequently than a stage curtain without being obtrusive. The fade-in or fade-out has conventionally been used to indicate some interruption in the passage of time, usually a long one. In Robert Mulligan's *To Kill a Mockingbird,* slow fade-outs and fade-ins, as well as long dissolves, make the transitions from scene to scene fluid and deliberate, in keeping with the slow pace of the sleepy southern town. In Tony Richardson's *The Loneliness of the Long-Distance Runner,* by contrast a tight, tense movie with an inexorable progression from event to event, scene replaces scene abruptly, with neither dissolve nor fade-out, so that we are constantly reminded of the impingement of the past (revealed in jolting movement to prior events) on the present.

SOUND

For a while the innovation of sound provided the industry and directors with a novelty, which they proceeded to exploit at the expense of the visual. Not only was dialogue added, but all sorts of sound effects suddenly assaulted the moviegoer. Whereas the early silent pictures were accompanied by piano music, the development of soundtracks resulted in elaborate musical scores whose emotional impact was designed to parallel the effect of the picture on the screen. The effects of the early fascination with sound still linger on, especially in certain musical clichés. Indeed, certain musical motifs of excitement or apprehension still serve as a foreshadowing of events for which the audience must be steeled. The fascination with sound in many cases led also to a neglect of the acting techniques that had been developed previously and often to a paralysis of motion on the screen.

Gradually, film makers learned to exploit this new technological development and to restore a better balance between the aural and the visual. What had been "movies" were now called "talkies" (a term which has, quite appropriately, given

His raising pigeons reveals Terry Malloy's capacity for tenderness and embryonic humanity; the fence of the enclosure reveals, symbolically, the barrier between him and Edie Doyle, in this rooftop scene from *On the Waterfront*.

way to the more visual term "movies"), but more had been added than dialogue. For a time the nature of the mechanical equipment meant that actors had to stay close to the recording microphone, which was often ingeniously concealed in a vase or a telephone. Technical improvements soon freed them as the mike became airborne, suspended above the actors' heads.

Dialogue was not the only element in the new aural convention. Sound effects had been used for years on the stage and were readily transferred to the screen. The fascination with music was another matter; the film makers still abhor a vacuum and silence is an exception in almost any film.

The sound in Elia Kazan's *On the Waterfront* is designed to support the action. The whistles from the boats on the river, the early morning noises along the docks, the soft noises of pigeons, all these are natural and effective. At times, even the director was content to have no background sound at all. Scenes in the film that were played against silence seem particularly effective.

There is no denying the power of music to suggest and to augment an emotional mood in keeping with the action on the screen. Yet the music may be obtrusive, and oddly enough, especially when it is too good. For the quality of the music may force its attention on the spectator engaged in the action. In *Fantasia,* Walt Disney, that master of the animated color cartoon, illustrated such magnificent works as Stravinsky's *The Rite of Spring* and Beethoven's *Pastoral* symphony and left the spectator torn between two media, unable to give his full attention to both at once.

In his book *The Joy of Music,* Leonard Bernstein, who composed the music for *On the Waterfront,* discusses the role of sound in that movie. He notes how the sound men . . .

> . . . may be told to keep the audience unconsciously aware of the traffic noise of a great city, yet they must also be aware of the sounds of wind and waves coming into a large, almost empty church *over* these traffic noises. And meantime the pedaling of a child's bicycle going around the church must punctuate the dialogue of two stray characters who have wandered in. Not a word of that dialogue, of course, must be lost, and the voices at the same time must arouse the dim echoes they would have in so cavernous a setting. And at this particular point no one (except the composer) has even begun to think how the musical background can fit in.[4]

Bernstein continues, more concretely,

> . . . there is, in *On the Waterfront,* a tender, hesitant love scene on the roof between the inarticulate hero and the un-

[4] Leonard Bernstein, *The Joy of Music* (New York, Simon and Schuster, 1959), p. 66.

inhibited heroine, surrounded by cooing pigeons. It was deliberately underwritten, and there are long, Kazan-like pauses between the lines—an ideal spot, it would seem, for the composer to take over. I suggested that here I should write love music that was shy at first and then, with growing, *Tristanish* intensity, come to a great climax which swamps the scene and screen, even drowning out the last prosaic bits of dialogue, which went something like this:

> "Have a beer with me?"
> (Very long pause)
> "Uh-huh." [5]

The music here was to do the real storytelling, and Kazan and company agreed enthusiastically, deciding to do it this way before even one note was written. So it was written, so orchestrated, so recorded.

But then . . . Kazan decided he just couldn't give up that ineffably sacred grunt which Brando emits at the end; it was, he thought, perhaps the two most eloquent syllables the actor had delivered in the whole script. And what happened to the music? As it mounts to its great climax, as the theme goes higher and higher and brasses and percussion join in with the strings and woodwinds, the all-powerful control dials are turned, and the sound fades out in a slow *diminuendo*. . . .

But there are musical compensations for the composer. He

. . . sees how the score has helped to blend atmospheres, to provide continuity, or to add a dimension by telling an inner story not overtly articulated in the dialogue or the action. For a score, judiciously applied to a film, can infuse it with a warm breath of its own, while one bar too many of music can be a serious detriment. [6]

For Bernstein, *West Side Story* represented an opportunity to translate a musical comedy into cinema. The opening

[5] *Ibid.*, p. 68.
[6] *Ibid.*, p. 69.

When Maria, in *West Side Story*, wails over the body of Tony, the two rival gangs of the Sharks and the Jets are drawn up on either side, forming a tableau which indicates the careful choreography of the entire movie.

minutes of the film combine music, color, and visual beauty, capitalizing on the resources of the movie camera. We see New York from high above the city in a series of panoramic shots: the United Nations Buildings, Yankee Stadium, Columbia University, a complex mesh of freeways and interchanges, skyscraper towers, tenements on the west side. Then the camera swoops down to a shot of the Jets, a local gang, snapping their fingers; the musical tempo begins to augment the visual story. Not a word of dialogue is spoken, but the choreography of Jerome Robbins makes the narrative very clear. As the rival gang of Sharks enters the choreographed motion, we have a vibrant and fast-paced chase in a series of short sequences, comic, inherently dangerous, foreboding.

69

The most dramatic musical sound effect comes near the end of the film. Maria asks Chino if Tony is safe. Since Tony has impulsively killed her brother in the Jets-Sharks rumble, the camera close-up of Chino captures a tormented, fist-marked, hate-filled, loving but unloved, uncomprehending boy whose shriek, "He killed your brother," comes at the close of a musical crescendo. *West Side Story* earned ten Academy Awards; one of these awards recognized the power of music to enhance the pace and artistry of this motion picture.

NEW TECHNIQUES

The particular shape of the conventional movie screen—a rectangle whose proportions are approximately 4 to 3—resulted from the choice of the frame size for the original negative. Camera aperture, projector aperture, and hence the actual screen in movie houses were constructed to the same ratio.

The decision on the proportion of 4 to 3 was not an arbitrary one. It may have been influenced by the fact that early motion pictures were exhibited in stores which were long and narrow. It was based on the mores of the day. This proportion was the concept in the art world. Stages too were designed in this way. For its period, this proportion was aesthetically most pleasing and most adaptable. Thomas Edison, who sold more motion picture equipment than anyone else, made his film size and screen size four by three. It became the worldwide standard.

That the rectangle constructed on a ratio of 4 to 3 might not necessarily be either aesthetic or entirely practical occurred to a number of film makers in Europe and the United States. Their early interest was abruptly sidetracked by the introduction of sound in 1928, an innovation unfolding so many potentialities that other changes were temporarily forgotten.

By 1930 interest was again directed to a consideration of the basic shape of the screen, especially of the aesthetic implications. While some argued for an increase in rectangularity, Sergei Eisenstein and others argued for the square, maintaining that it allowed more flexibility in the range of horizontal and vertical images. Their discussion never passed the stage of speculation. The costs indicated in changing the shape of film frame, camera and projector aperture, and movie screen were extraordinary, and when the great crash of 1929 finally caught up with the hitherto depression-proof movie industry in 1931, such considerations were abandoned.

In 1952 the first of a series of radical innovations appeared when an independent group developed a process of filming called Cinerama. It was an instant success. Using three lenses and as many as six separate microphones, the process recorded an arc of vision almost half a circle; so that much of what the eye sees only peripherally was recorded too.

Projected onto a giant curving screen, with sound supplied by as many as eight speakers, the image tended to engulf the viewer and draw him into the action as no image had ever done before. The process was, and is, costly. The three lenses each exposed different negatives; when projected onto a wide screen, the best of synchronization still left occasional "seams" between the images. And Cinerama had to own and operate cameras, projectors, and theatres, because the cost of installation was so high—$75,000 per theatre in some cases.

The allure of gadgetry was well demonstrated in 1953 when an attempt at creating three-dimensional movies called VistaVision equipped each viewer with special stereopticon glasses (for the most part given to the viewer) and showed him a startlingly lifelike movie called *Bwana Devil*.[7]

A flurry of movies that used the stereopticon technique followed, all capitalizing on the power of the method to draw the spectator into his 3-D world. Content frequently suffered; the industry exploited gadgets at the expense of quality. So

[7] Arthur Knight, *The Liveliest Art* (New York, Macmillan, 1957), p. 314.

satiated was the spectator with the technique that by the time quality films were produced by that method, he stayed away or went to see movies in conventional releases.

In 1952 Twentieth Century Fox developed a process that registered a wide picture on a standard 35 mm. film, using a special camera and projector lens developed years earlier in France by Dr. Henri Chrétien. This camera lens, designated anamorphic, squeezed twice the information into a smaller area in the film; in the theatre this information was again expanded for a screen twice as wide as the normal screen. The viewer needed no glasses and experienced a third dimensional effect. Theatre owners were pleased; they could use existing theatre projection facilities; they needed only a special lens, stereophonic sound, and a wide screen. Furthermore, on September 16, 1953, Twentieth Century Fox issued as its first production a quality movie, *The Robe,* and CinemaScope was in. Today nearly all theatres are equipped to show Cinema-Scope type movies.

The trend toward large size screens in the theatres forced many producers into using films wider than the standard 35 mm. with the hope of maintaining picture sharpness. The use of a wider film almost invariably means complete retooling of equipment, as well as of projectors and screens; and of the various experimenters, only the flamboyant Michael Todd's Todd-AO process, developed by Dr. O'Brien of the American Optical Company, survives at the moment. Todd-AO uses a curving screen and a stereophonic sound projector. Its single 65 mm. film means a wide single image and no trouble synchronizing multiple reels on several projectors.

The success of Todd-AO was demonstrated by his opulent *Around the World in 80 Days.* The wide screen, the color, the startling panorama the screen made possible, the direction, an ingenious use of cartoons during the credits, and the acting of David Niven and Cantinflas combined to make fine entertainment and fine film.

Many techniques have now stretched the screen out of its original proportions of 4 to 3, yet the increased width makes its own demands. It provides opportunities for increased artistry. Neither is size necessarily a virtue. The giant screen can successfully encompass a mountain range, or an iceberg, but a close-up of an embrace, a face, or an ear may become simply grotesque. Of course that may be what the director seeks.

When technical innovation is wedded to aesthetic considerations and the shape of the screen can be manipulated so that it best accommodates the image which it reflects, in size as well as dimension, the moviemaker will still be following the lead established by the great innovator D. W. Griffith, who accomplished much the same thing by imaginative photography.

Today, directors like Tony Richardson are reexploiting old techniques and developing new ones, capable of enhancing any development like CinemaScope or Todd-AO, by an imaginative use of masks, used either while shooting or while cutting. In the exuberant *Tom Jones,* for example, the director uses the mask as if he were using curtains to close a scene that modesty forbids us to watch. Richardson employs a variety of comparable optical effects which were developed in the silent films and which reinforce the picture's extraordinary force. Among these are "freezing" the picture into tableaux at crises of violent action and "irising out" to concentrate attention on an impish facial expression at the conclusion of a scene.

When innovations and experiment are coupled with courage, imagination, taste, and vitality, as they have been by such directors as Tony Richardson, the results are bound to be exciting; here, the means are subordinated to the end.

The art of movie making, like any art, has its own conventions, some of which it has borrowed from the stage and further developed. Most cinematic conventions have resulted directly from the technical development of the camera, the refinement of the photographic process to include color and a soundtrack, and later experiments with the size and shape of the image. Criticism of film as an art form must consider and evaluate these conventions as exploited by the sensibility of the director.

CHAPTER FIVE

The Movie in the English Program

THE FILM ON LITERATURE

A medium that has had such an impact upon our culture and can command such attention from the spectator, has a variety of uses within the classroom, ranging from the showing of a documentary for informational purposes, to the showing of a full-length film in a unit devoted to the study of motion pictures as motion pictures. The documentary can furnish "instant information" about an author, period, or country. It is problematical whether such information will immediately increase the perception and understanding of the text, normally the major concern of the English teacher, or whether indeed it will increase the skill of the reader. Yet it can motivate and entertain and lend variety to the program; in addition, the proper documentary may establish a desirable mood or atmosphere for further study of the literature for which the documentary is peripheral material.

Material excerpted from a full-length motion picture may be quite another matter. That there might be a wealth of material available for educational purposes from a large number of theatrical motion pictures first occurred to a number of educators in 1937. By the academic year 1938-1939, the Motion Picture Association of America had sponsored a nonprofit, educational corporation, Teaching Film Custodians, Inc., whose task it has been to examine significant motion picture materials and make them available, without any financial return to the cooperating producing companies. Their

Courtesy of the Rank Organization

Sets, costumes, and skillful staging characterize Olivier's work, as in this scene in which Hamlet hopes "to catch the conscience of the king" by presenting the murder of Gonzago, "The Mouse-trap," to the guilty Claudius.

cooperative program of educational service and public relations makes available a number of excerpts of full-length films to educational institutions and systems at a nominal cost.

Several dozen such excerpts are presently available, drawn from feature films based on novels or plays. In some instances the excerpts are made from several films, as for example *Understanding Movies,* or *Charles Dickens: Characters in Action.* Like these, many excerpts have been made in cooperation with a committee from the National Council of Teachers of English, including *Kipling's India* (made from *Kim*), *Meet the Forsytes* (from *That Forsyte Woman*), *Washington Square* (from *The Heiress*), and *Pygmalion.* An excerpt made from Olivier's *Henry V,* called *Shakespeare's Theater,* shows the exterior and interior of the Globe Theatre of about 1600, its

76

The opening scenes of *Henry V* are shot in a reconstruction of the Globe Theatre. Here the apron, inner and upper stages, gallery, and the gallants seated on the apron, are clearly visible.

stage, its galleries, its audience, and the preparations backstage for a performance.

The excerpts are accompanied by guides, prepared by the committee of teachers who helped prepare the excerpts themselves. These guides are available upon request, and the teacher should familiarize himself with them before showing the film to the class. Then he will be in a better position to judge just how the excerpt is to be used.

One advantage of such excerpts is that they are not only available in 16 mm. film, and hence can be screened in most classrooms or audiovisual libraries with appropriate equipment, but they are short enough so that they will fit comfortably into the conventional class period. It is probably wise to allow no more than thirty minutes for a classroom viewing of any film, leaving adequate time for discussion or for introduction. Most TFC excerpts are designed to run from ten to twenty minutes. The short excerpt has the further virtue of leaving the choice of when to view the film to the discretion of the teacher, who remains in charge of the class period.

The teacher may wish to show the excerpt first, before an assignment is given, in order to introduce the novel or play, catch the imagination of the student, and arouse his curiosity. He may wish to wait until the student is well into the work assigned in order to show what a first-rate imagination has done in adapting the material from literature to the moving picture medium. It would be well to emphasize the fact that the moving picture is *not* the book, nor the excerpt the movie, any more than a paraphrase of a poem is the poem itself. If we agree with our premise as stated earlier, that form is inseparable from content in any art form, we shall avoid a number of critical pitfalls which await the student too willing to criticize a film simply because it is not "faithful" to the novel, as if it were possible for one form to be faithful to another. The movie, as movie, must be criticized on its own merits, as suggested earlier, but a novel may still serve as a useful springboard into a movie, and vice versa.

The excerpt from the feature motion picture *Pygmalion* may be used in the English classroom for a variety of objectives. The excerpt itself was prepared by a committee of the National Council of Teachers of English, in close cooperation with TFC. The film, the first to be made from Shaw's plays, with Shaw's blessing, won the Academy Award for the Best Screen Play of 1939. Produced by Gabriel Pascal, it was directed jointly by Anthony Asquith and Leslie Howard, who also played the part of Henry Higgins.

The film follows the events of the play and uses much of the same dialogue. The romantic ending is left much less ambiguous than is the ending of the play. (Shaw's subsequent Epilogue left little doubt that Shaw himself found a happy ending—i.e., a marriage between Eliza and Higgins—most unlikely, and most inartistic). Besides, one major scene, central to the development is added. In Shaw's own words,

> As to *Pygmalion,* the scene in which Eliza makes her successful debut at the Ambassador's party was the root of the play at its inception. But when I got to work I left it to the imagination of the audience, as the theatre could not afford its expense and it made the play too long.
>
> Sir James Barrie spotted this at once and remonstrated. So when the play was screened, I added the omitted scene, as the cinema can afford practically unlimited money, and the absence of intervals [intermissions] left plenty of time to spare.[1]

In the English classroom, the excerpt might well be used in connection with a study of Shaw and his writings, of *Pygmalion,* and of other plays as well. It may be used, for example, to develop the use of myth, or theme, central to many different treatments; it may serve for a study of the artistry of film; it may serve as the basis for original student writing. It raises the question of social mobility. It is very much concerned with linguistics.

As an approach to a study of G. B. Shaw, the excerpt may be studied in order to demonstrate the extraordinary skill of Shaw as a playwright. In a very few lines of dialogue, Shaw has accomplished what is always one of the major tasks facing the writer: the exposition of the problem and the introduction of the major figures. The opening sequence in the Covent Garden Market introduces us in rapid succession to Eliza, the Cockney flower girl, Professor Higgins, Colonel Pickering, Freddie, his mother, and his sister. The conflict between the upper class and the lower is immediate. The sets, as well as the dialects, make apparent the great distance between Eliza's

---

[1] Hayden Church, Interview with Bernard Shaw on "How to Write a Play," Glasgow *Evening Times,* February 7, 1939, in Archibald Henderson, *George Bernard Shaw: Man of the Century* (New York, Appleton-Century-Crofts, 1956), p. 730.

station in life and the world of Freddie, his mother, and Professor Higgins—a world whose eminence is distinguished primarily by speech.

Not only do Shaw's *Pygmalion* and his other plays furnish much material for the English classroom, but his prefaces, sequels, and essays, provocative, fresh, and polemic, are a source for a unit within the English curriculum that could employ the TFC excerpt.

Even a brief encounter with the excerpt can serve to teach the student much about film artistry. The opening scene already cited is an excellent translation into visual images of conflicts and situations described in dialogue or stage directions. The editing in the opening sequence is especially skillful. Differences in station are emphasized through crosscutting and close-up, as well as dialogue. The soaring pillars of Inigo Jones' architecture contrast ironically with the bedraggled figure of Eliza huddled at their base.

One of the most successful interpolations occurs when Professor Higgins embarks upon Eliza's training. Where the play has simply made references to the process, the film invades Professor Higgins' laboratory, a place filled with interesting and intricate apparatus. In one memorable scene the camera is trained on a match, gaslight, spinning disks, mirrors, an oscilloscope, a large model of an ear, and finally Professor Higgins and Colonel Pickering. As the camera retreats to a longer shot, the human actors become smaller and smaller and the room is dominated by an enormous loudspeaker.

In another sequence after the professor has been training Eliza, the film dissolves from the actual lessons to the effect the lessons have had on Eliza by picturing the sleeping, restless girl thrashing about as she relives the painful efforts of Professor Higgins to exact letter-perfect performances from her. The sleeping girl, tossing and turning, is juxtaposed with the details of her lessons. In one sequence Professor Higgins asks Eliza to repeat a series of sounds while holding three marbles in her mouth. When she swallows one, he allays her alarm and graciously assures her that he has more marbles. The scenes offer the camera an opportunity to probe the laboratory details; we see in turn the phonograph, the loudspeaker, and other intricate and elaborate pieces of apparatus. In one sequence, shots are very quickly spaced to give the impression of mounting tension. The pressure of practice, of the professor's exacting demands, continues into another scene showing Eliza tossing in bed while alternate shots show Higgins wagging a finger at her, saying, "Bad! Bad! Bad!" This scene finally focuses on the girl, no longer asleep, sitting on a chair, weeping. After she is placated the film shows us Higgins, shouting "No! No! No!"—punctuating each "No" by pounding his fist on the table and glaring at her. Perhaps the most amusing and telling sequence in the training scenes occurs with very little dialogue. We see Eliza studying, repeating Higgins' instructions, Mrs. Pearce remonstrating with Higgins, "It's 3 A.M.," and Colonel Pickering, supine on the sofa, snoring.

The triumphant presentation at the Ambassador's reception, the scene described by Shaw himself earlier in this chapter, the pomp and pageantry of the affair are natural material for the camera to exploit. In one particular shot the procession is seen reflected in a mirror with a highly decorated, ornate, and opulent frame. The artificiality and elegance of the scene are symbolized by a shot possible only in the moving picture.

Indeed throughout the entire excerpt there is opportunity for the student to note and comment on the functions of editing, of camera angle, of set and costume, of music, acting, and characterization.

From another point of view entirely, the excerpt itself may raise fundamental questions of social mobility and the conflict of values inevitable in an attempt to rise above one's station. In the play such an attempt is seen eventually as futile. In the movie, "Fetch me my slippers, Eliza," (not in the excerpt) is sufficient evidence for the audience to assume a happy ending. The musical *My Fair Lady* left no doubt.

For those interested in linguistics, the emphasis on dialect serves as a springboard for a number of considerations of the importance of speech in daily affairs. Dialect and its accompanying grammatical idiosyncrasies serve the writer and screenwriter alike as means to establish locale, social position, and breeding; dialect also provides an easy means for stereotyping character. Perhaps, until the student can see *Pygmalion* well-acted or well-filmed, even in excerpt, its value in the study of speech as a mark of education and background or the possibilities of corrective instruction and the patterning of English sound-types might well be lost.

Encyclopaedia Britannica Films, Inc., offers a series of filmed lessons in the humanities, which present major literary works within the frame of the culture and the age which produced them. Each series comprises four lessons, each consisting of a film of about thirty minutes' duration. The remainder of the period is used for class question and discussion from material supplied by EBF.

These films were originally prepared by the Council for a Television Course in the Humanities for Secondary Schools, Inc., with Floyd Rinker as Executive Director. They were filmed by Encyclopaedia Britannica Films, Inc. The series presents Thornton Wilder's *Our Town,* with Clifton Fadiman lecturing; Sophocles' *Oedipus Rex,* using Bernard Knox's translation and under Knox's lectureship; and *Hamlet,* with Maynard Mack, a Yale professor and Shakespearean authority, lecturing.

These filmed lessons are carefully prepared and skillfully edited. Within the scope of the four lessons, the films attempt to place the work within some chronological and sociological framework and (with the exception of *Our Town*) to illustrate the lecture by frequent use of scenes acted from the plays. The first lecture is a general introduction to the age and the work. Subsequent lectures present the substance of the play. The dramas are performed by the Stratford Shakespearean Festival Foundation of Canada.

In the series on *Hamlet,* Maynard Mack begins by discussing the Age of Elizabeth, an age marked by strong leadership and equally strong individualism. The terms *Elizabethan* and *Shakespearean* are almost synonymous historically, and Professor Mack illustrates his opening introductory lecture with scenes from *Henry VIII* and other plays. While the camera focuses on a model of the Globe Theatre, designed by C. Walter Hodges, Professor Mack talks about the heterogeneous audience and the relationship between the kind of theatre and the kind of play presented there.

The next three lessons, each twenty-eight minutes in length, are entitled *What Happens in Hamlet, The Poisoned Kingdom,* and *The Readiness Is All.* The sections of the play which are dramatized are ably acted by the Stratford Players; we are swiftly made aware of the problem facing Hamlet and his desire for revenge, in the second film. In the third, Maynard Mack traces the theme of poison through the imagery of the play. In the last, he discusses the three tragic problems Hamlet encounters—the reality of evil, the uncertainty of appearances, and the inevitability of death. In every case his general thesis is illustrated by reference to the text of the play, insofar as it has been dramatized by the players who appear.

The advantages of such films are many. With the films comes a guide for teachers, furnishing a vast amount of material for class discussion including questions, historical data, and vocabulary. Each film assumes little or no prior knowledge on the part of the students as to the period, the genre, or the play. In the study of *Hamlet,* Professor Mack offers no single critical interpretation and leaves the business of close textual analysis hopefully up to the individual instructor and his class.

There are several disadvantages, which may be characteristic of any film which hopes to introduce such literary works to a wide and heterogeneous audience of secondary school students in this century. The opening lectures are designed to give an overview of the period and of drama in general; they sometimes succeed in being patronizing, especially to classes that have had some experience in literature. The later lectures in each series are more specific, more useful, and closer to the text.

More recently, the Encyclopaedia Britannica Series includes films on Athens, Aristotle, Greek Lyric Poetry, Art, Chartres, and the novel, with particular emphasis on *Great Expectations*. Such distinguished attempts to preserve on film the efforts of fine scholars and experienced companies mark a step forward in the use of modern media to teach.

THE FILM AND LITERARY TECHNIQUE

A unit on satire may fall within the legitimate confines of the English course accustomed to dealing with American or English literature on a chronological basis. It assumes, of course, a shift in emphasis from historical information about types and authors to a concern with the meaning of what is read. Such a unit, properly arranged, allows an individual teacher great flexibility of choice in the selection of material, whether arranged chronologically, topically, or by genre. The nature of satire is such that the reader must sustain a special critical awareness of tone and attitude; he must be alert to a number of different kinds of irony, differing in subtlety; he must be able to identify the character of the speaker. The close reading of satiric material demands an attention to the functions of language beyond that of narrative or of expository prose.

For several reasons the showing of short films in the course of studying satire will strengthen the ability of the reader to detect irony in prose. At the same time a kind of double reinforcement will take place, so that the reader's ability to detect subtlety and significance in the visual image will be increased. Visual irony operates on the same principle as verbal irony but is sometimes more immediately apparent.

The primary tool of the satirist is irony, which always makes a demand on the inexperienced reader. In its simplest manifestation irony may appear simply as a reversal of direction within a statement. Just as Antony's word *honorable* in Shakespeare's *Julius Caesar* is used ironically by the time he has repeated it three times, so most ironic statements appear so only in context. By its nature, irony is apparent only in terms of larger meanings and whole contexts. When Lennox reviews Macbeth's conduct in killing the "delinquents" who guarded Duncan the night he was murdered, he asks,

> Was that not nobly done? Ay, and wisely, too;
> For 'twould have angered any heart alive
> To hear the men deny't.

The words *nobly* and *wisely* are ironic, in keeping with the entire speech, but Lennox's position is not at once apparent, and only an examination of the entire speech and situation will enable the student to savor the quality of individual words and phrases.

The techniques which Swift employed in *Gulliver's Travels* not only are ironic but include the allegorical and the symbolic as well. The great care with which he develops the Lilliputians on the scale of 1/12th of Gulliver's size is finally seen as used to construct a physical equivalent to their moral size as, petty and ungrateful, they threaten to blind that person whose vision describes them to us and to the world. This world is described to us in *visual* terms; the difference between Gulliver's vision and ours is one principle of satire.

In "A Modest Proposal," the shock value is fully realized only when the student, appalled at the proposal for devouring one-year-old children and hence solving the problems of over-population, unemployment, and lack of food all at once, realizes that the proposal is symbolic. Not only are we incapable of providing a more humane and rational solution than this, but in effect the English are already devouring the poor.

Satire as a mode of writing exists in every period and in every country. From Aristophanes to E. B. White, the possibilities of social criticism (and literary criticism, through parody) have appealed to most major writers. In our own time such works as Orwell's *Animal Farm* employ devices ranging from simple irony ("All animals are equal, but some are more equal than others") to allegory (In Lord Dunsany's version of "The Hare and the Tortoise," the forest is menaced by a terrible forest fire which threatens to destroy the entire population. The animals need to get word around fast, and they send the tortoise.).

Satire as literary criticism often appears as parody. Perhaps nowhere else is indirection so effective as when it is used to dispose of bad writing, and John Updike's take-off on Kerouac's *On the Road* reveals the essential adolescent quality of Kerouac's writing when Updike describes a scooter and tricycle as suitable vehicles for his children in "On the Sidewalk," and concludes,

> . . . But I was not allowed to cross the street. I stood on the gray curb thinking, They said I could cross it when I grew up, and what do they mean grown up? I'm thirty-nine now, and felt sad.[2]

The National Film Board of Canada has produced and licensed for distribution a short, twelve-minute color cartoon, *The Romance of Canadian Transportation,* which appears on

[2] John Updike, "On the Sidewalk (After Reading, at Long Last, 'On the Road' by Jack Kerouac)," *The New Yorker,* February 21, 1959, p. 32.

first viewing to be purely informational. It opens with a shot of an aviator running out of gas and subsequently parachuting down into a crowded intersection where, enshrouded by his parachute, he succeeds in backing up traffic for miles. The film abruptly shifts to early North America and the first British explorers. Ostensibly, the film is a history of the development of transportation in Canada and proceeds to describe the early canoe, the bateau (from the French *bateau*), the oxcart, the sled (in winter), the stagecoach, the sailing ship, the train, the internal combustion engine, the airplane, and ultimately the flying saucer.

At each stage of development, the voice of the narrator, ever bland, proceeds to herald the onset of the next invention with controlled chamber-of-commerce excitement. The announcement is couched entirely in cliché, and it is only when the words of the announcer are contrasted with the visual images on the screen that the intent of the film maker becomes obvious.

For example, the advent of the traders, we are told, "taxed all existing facilities." On the screen we are shown a picture of a canoe, sinking slowly below the surface of the river under the weight of hides. "Passengers traveled in relative comfort," we are told, and on the screen the businessman is shown thrown from seat to roof to wall as the stagecoach travels along. "The face of Canada was changed," intones the narrator, and on the screen we see the passengers of the first Canadian railroad, blackened by the smoke from the locomotive. "Canada moves forward to keep its rendezvous with destiny," and on the screen appears the intersection which was the scene of the original first shot, all traffic at a standstill. Overhead hovers a flying saucer, whose occupant emerges, takes one horrified look at the chaos below him and retreats to Mars.

The devices available for the literary satirist—irony, accentuation, exaggeration—are all present in this film and are peculiarly effective. The cartoonist is in an unusually favorable position to render such distortion, by virtue of his medium; color and line, as well as an arbitrary choice of scene to juxtapose against scene, are his tools. The abstraction "obstacle" can be rendered concrete and tangible, in the form of the Rockies. Line and color are stylized to a degree which was then (1957) unknown in cartoons, but has recently been exploited in cartoons by such innovators as those artists who draw Colonel Bullwinkle in *Rocky and His Friends.* At the same time, the accompanying music can serve either as ironic counterpoint or as reinforcement of the clichés of the announcer. The attempt to provoke a lethargic ox into movement is accompanied by a passage from the blues; a shot of the Rockies is supported by a motif from western folk music; the early wood-burning train, wending its way across the prairies, is accompanied by boogie-woogie. The contemporary scenes are underscored by jazz.

In short, the juxtaposition of words against image and image against sound succeeds in being ironic. The film as a whole serves as a comment on all progress, as the entire transportation system of a community—car, train, and boat— grinds to a cacophonous halt in the center of things. "Romance" itself is ultimately satiric.

In a different mood and tone is another short film. Produced by the Boston Museum of Fine Arts and the Fogg Museum, a short (twenty-five-minute) film called *The Follies of the Town* provides more instant information about eighteenth century London than do a dozen novels. The visual ingredient of the film is drawn from the works of Hogarth. The camera never, however, shows an entire painting but concentrates on one part or another from the various series including *The Rake's Progress, The Whore's Progress, Marriage à la Mode,* and the two works called *Gin Lane* and *Beer Lane,* as well as others. We see small portions of each of the series, returning again and again to the same picture, never seeing the whole.

The effect is that of a documentary of eighteenth century London, complete with smells and sounds.

The narration, except for an occasional introductory or summarizing remark, consists entirely of passages read from Johnson, Smollett, Swift, Fielding, Steele, Defoe, Goldsmith, and Boswell. The musical accompaniment is harpsichord—Handel and Scarlatti.

The effect of the narration is an uncompromising description of London in all its energy and squalor. The effect of the musical underscoring is ironic; the delicate and controlled, highly genteel music is in violent contrast to the scenes of poverty and degradation, disease and crime, which Hogarth portrayed.

The visual effect is most striking. Accustomed as we are to responding to movement, we are only momentarily aware that we are seeing moving pictures of drawings and that only the camera is moving. Because we see only one part of any picture, we may move across it or shift abruptly to another picture entirely. For instance, on one occasion the camera is studying that picture in *The Rake's Progress* where the mother brings in her betrayed daughter and confronts the Rake. The camera moves in on the hand of the mother—pointing to the belly of the daughter. On another occasion the subject is not the corruption of young girls by the nobility but the high incidence of crime among the poor; the camera returns to the scene already described above, but to another part, where a wizened servant is in the act of helping himself to his master's open purse.

In the course of his narration, the speaker succeeds in communicating a total impression of the noise, energy, filth, poverty, vice, exuberance, and extraordinary vitality of eighteenth-century London. The shots, chosen to illustrate the prose sequences, are not always pleasant and have the same frankness and abruptness that we associate with Fielding, Defoe, or Boswell. They are rescued from being mere documentary by Hogarth's extraordinary comic vision, tempered as it is with compassion. His faces are original, often distorted, sometimes diseased. The human body is sharply delineated, sometimes grotesque. If not distorted or diseased it is often represented as maimed, as if from war or accident. Distortions of this kind are a characteristic Hogarth touch, as if the physical appearance were representative of some inner moral ugliness as well as symbolic of the degeneracy of a society which tolerates poverty and crime and thrives on war.

A final satiric comment is supplied by the ever present dog, a Hogarth signature, supplying emphasis, ironic underscoring, or contrast to the human plights represented. These details, all visual, are devices which correspond to those verbal ones available to the satirist but are more immediate and more compelling, if occasionally repellent.

The contemporary scene provides the subject matter for Francis Thompson's *New York*. This fifteen-minute color film uses a number of experimental techniques to achieve a tour de force of visual impression, supported by a brilliant sound track which, like many of the sequences in the film, is lyric and satiric at the same time, appropriate enough for an age of such complexity and ambiguity as our own. The camera covers a day in the life of a "cliff-dweller" in Manhattan. There is no commentary or dialogue. The setting is established aurally at first with several blasts from a tugboat whistle. A shot of George Washington Bridge, blurred and shot from a low angle, with lights reflecting in the water, images of cranes, girders, and buildings, finally gives way to a close-up of buildings, then of windows, repeated and repeated in multiple images. The camera holds on an alarm clock, a single exposure shot which explodes into action as the alarm goes off and the day begins.

The subject of the film is the hurry, press, and confusion of the city dweller. The principal technique is the multiple image caught by the multiple-faceted lens of Francis Thompson, explicitly and symbolically revealing that the city dweller is but one of hundreds of people following the same daily pattern. Windows, buildings, cars, and buses are also revealed, repeated endlessly across the screen in patterns which shift and reform as the camera moves.

A continuing technique, the blurred focus, when coupled with the first, succeeds in suggesting the breathlessness and dizzying pace of city life. It is particularly effective in the evening scenes, as the camera moves down an avenue of marquees under the blaze of Broadway at night.

Thompson has borrowed a trick from the photographer Weegee and from the old trick mirrors in the sideshows, in order to distort images. Shooting reflections in various curved surfaces, he can make monsters out of buses and automobiles. Watching the feet of the hurrying noontime crowd, the camera becomes surrealistic and shows feet moving, always in multiple image, attached to legs which become knees which become legs and feet upside down from the first—a visual comment on the dehumanizing and endless procession of shoes on pavement.

Each sequence proceeds from a fairly recognizable, though somewhat distorted opening sequence, through greater and greater distortion until it becomes almost nonrepresentational. In evening scenes, for example, the lights increase in intensity and become increasingly blurred; the spectrum of evening colors in New York becomes increasingly insistent and overpowering. A ballet dancer is multiplied into a chorus line; a visit to a nightclub focuses on the instruments which, blurred and distorted, dominate the screen. Each image is accompanied by its appropriate musical comment; the bell of a trumpet swells as it blares; a keyboard in black and white writhes in time to the piano music; a drum obbligato becomes a pure orgiastic explosion of abstract pattern on the screen.

In the process of multiplying, distorting, and abstracting his images, Thompson is making his own ambiguous statement about the emotional impact of twentieth-century city life on this planet. At times the scenes are lyrical, at times ironic. Many shots have a Mondrianlike quality which emphasizes the mathematical and engineering skill of modern man. Many shots emphasize the submergence of individuality in the crowd. All shots emphasize the enormous pace and restlessness of a dynamic city. The theme is motion, and the moving picture is the ideal medium for its expression here.

The color cartoon, the photographing of drawings with a motion picture camera, and the exploitation of all the possibilities of photographing city life with multiple-faceted lenses, reflecting surfaces, and a nervous and peripatetic camera, represent only various possibilities in the entire range of short films available through various commercial outlets. Each film mentioned above is excellent in its own way, and each film has its own poetic, sociological, satiric, or thematic contribution to make to an English program or to other programs, for that matter, whether in art or social science.

A unit on satire enables the instructor to select, for close reading and discussion, works from an extraordinarily wide range of cultures and periods. His own bent may be literary or historical; his concern must be first with technique—with style, with attitude, with detail, with the relation of part to whole, with order and sequence—in short with structure. An examination of a film in connection with a unit on satire by its very definition requires an analysis of film as film. Such an analysis should reinforce close reading techniques and result in more intelligent viewing of films.

CHAPTER SIX

Analysis of
a Film Classic

THE FILM AS A UNIT

The usual classroom period does not allow a teacher to present a film of one- to two-hour duration, but occasionally students will see a whole film under controlled educational conditions (at an auditorium film session or other showing outside of class hours), and often students will see a whole film at a commercial theatre or on television.

In this chapter, a complete film, Orson Welles' *Citizen Kane,* will be examined from a number of aspects. By the testimony of many critics and film makers, it is a classic because of its ingenious use of filmic techniques put to serious purpose. In depicting the rise of a newspaper tycoon whose life in some respects parallels that of William Randolph Hearst, it makes valuable statements about journalism and social responsibility.

RÉSUMÉ OF *CITIZEN KANE*

This two-hour film opens with a shot of a NO TRESPASSING sign at the entrance of Kane's run-down estate Xanadu, moves on to a lighted room in the castlelike mansion, observes in close-up two lips speaking the word "Rosebud," watches a paperweight globe containing artificial snow drop from a hand and bounce to the floor. A newsfilm documentary breaks in, its pictures accompanied by stentorian narration. Lasting eight and one-half minutes, it shows the rise and fall of news-

93

paper tycoon Charles Kane. In a darkened viewing room, the makers of the film documentary ask each other the meaning of "Rosebud." The rest of *Citizen Kane* follows a reporter as he studies a diary and interviews one of Kane's former wives and his two closest newspaper associates in an effort to decipher "Rosebud."

In a series of overlapping and purposefully repetitive flashbacks, Kane's life, his thirst for power, and his egotism are recreated in every sequence of shots. The picture ends with the reporter's visit to Xanadu and an inspection of objects from Kane's personal life and foreign travels which are stored there; the camera reveals the secret of "Rosebud" to the viewer but not to the reporter, who admits that there is much more to understanding a life than finding the meaning of one key word. The film ends with the sign NO TRESPASSING.

This film is essentially true to the eye's experience. With few exceptions, the pictures in *Citizen Kane* are authentic. The vast interiors of Xanadu, the costumes of the period, and the makeup of Joseph Cotten and Orson Welles (both young actors at the time) as old men are convincing. When the March of the News documentary portrays Kane's last days and speaks of his self-induced seclusion, the camera looks through a white wooden fence, which sometimes obstructs our view of the old man sitting in a wheelchair on the lawn of his estate. The way we see him is true to the way we see a public figure in real life. When the labor leader denounces Kane to a large crowd in the city square, he speaks in the short phrases and long pauses of a man using a loudspeaker in a great space, and an echo or feedback registers slightly as he talks. We do not see all of Kane's life, but the many shots and sequences we do see come at our ears and eyes truly.

Only two or three of the hundreds of shots in *Citizen Kane* seem artificial. The mock-up of Xanadu viewed from a distance at the beginning of the film does not look believable;

it seems borrowed from *Snow White and the Seven Dwarfs.*
The long shot of the shabby New York *Inquirer* building is
obviously a picture of a poorly painted drop.

In their most skillful use, the authentic images in this
film carry a symbolic meaning as well as a feeling of reality.
When the March of the News documentary ends, the film
projector and sound track come to a skidding, blurred *scronch*
that brings the viewer suddenly into the preview room with
the men who are making the documentary (telling us that
Kane is important enough to warrant having all these men
work on a film record of his life, and at the same time suggesting, because it comes after pictures of his death, that the great
man's life has ground ignominiously to a halt rather than ending in a burst in glory).

In this film the camera moves a great deal but seldom
merely as a trick. When Susan Alexander (Kane's second
wife) begins the opera career which Kane has forced on her,
we see her at stage center waiting for the curtain to go up, and
then, projected against the set behind her, the shadow of the
curtain rising. As our eyes follow the shadow up, the camera
keeps going, straight up through the flies, higher and higher
until we reach a scaffold, where stand two stagehands looking
down. One turns to the other and holds his nose. It is a slow
and auspicious rise to heights for a vulgarly expressed verdict.

Early in the story when the reporter hunts for Susan
Alexander, the camera finds a roadhouse in the rain, moves in
to examine a displayed outdoor painting of the blonde singer's
face, moves up to the roof and the name SUSAN ALEXANDER,
in lights, over the sign, down through a skylight to a Mondrianlike pattern of tables covered with white tablecloths,
empty except for one, where sits Susan, her head laid on her
folded arms, an empty glass in front of her. To look down on
her makes her seem even more forlorn. At other times the film
more often looks up at actors, particularly at Kane and his

two editorial associates, the camera shooting almost from ground level to increase their size and to build the feeling of power.

Again and again the film communicates visually rather than verbally, although it also employs narration in the news documentary and the device of friends recalling in words their memories (but only as a lead into pictorial narrative). The viewer does not find out the music critic's opinion of Susan Alexander's opera debut through a trite conversation with the man next to him in the audience, but he simply sees the performance on stage intercut with shots of the critic meticulously tearing up his program and bending it into a toy construction.

Near the end of the film, the world of Charles Foster Kane has become too big for him and no one needs to speak that truth, for the picture of Kane standing in the mouth of Xanadu's cavernous main fireplace—the opening at least two feet above his head—portrays a man small against the scale of life he has created for himself. Only a few seconds of this shot on the screen establish its meanings, as does a shot in the sequence which begins with Kane's suggestion to his wife that they have a beach party at Xanadu; the viewer sees a long string of black limousines moving slowly along the ocean's edge, like a funeral cortege. Nothing more is needed to show the monstrous distortion of the concept of play which Kane has brought about in his effort to manufacture life.

The film is like a Greek tragedy in its tension between foreknowledge and uncertainty. The news documentary with which it begins previews the life of Kane we are to see in the total film. But as that life is recapitulated in subsequent flashbacks, we feel a suspense just as we do at the unraveling of the puzzle of Oedipus the King in Sophocles' play, even though we know of his ultimate doom from our own foreknowledge. Seldom are we sure about how Kane or those close to him are going to act in any one situation.

Characteristic of this uncertainty is the sequence in which

Kane comes into the Chicago office of the *Inquirer* after his wife's singing debut. He is met by newsmen who assure him that all the reviews which are being written are favorable—except that they have not yet seen the review by Jed Leland, Kane's associate. Kane walks to the inner office, finds Jed at his desk, head sunken on his arms, bottle at his elbow, in his typewriter a half-finished review that begins with an uncomplimentary paragraph.

Kane takes the review, says he will finish it, and we suddenly see one typewriter key in microscopic close-up striking the paper: *w.* Then on the screen by itself, the letter *e* as it is struck, then *a,* then *k.* One letter comes at a time, and we have not seen any preceding words to help us guess what we are seeing. Viewing only one letter at a time, at first we think we are simply being shown that Kane is typing, but when all four letters have gone by, we remember, with effort, that we have seen the letters that make up the word *weak,* and we know that Kane is also panning his wife's performance, as we never expected him to do.

On every level the film is full of similar uncertainties and surprises that give rise to an electric feeling of reality. Persons seldom say what the viewer expects; they speak humorously in serious situations; they cast ambiguous looks at each other and at the camera. On an ocean liner docked from Europe just before the outbreak of World War I, Kane jokes professionally with the interviewing reporter; then drawing himself up, he looks at the newsreel camera and says expansively, "You can take my word for it. There will be no war."

The overall unity of the picture is achieved by a play of opposites against each other. It moves in a series of rushing blasts, begun with the hammerlike blows of the news documentary, which is modeled on the old *March of Time* film technique, and further broken by constant flashbacks, which repeat and fill out the life of Kane as the persons close to him retell it. The story line is thus broken and truncated again and again before it is finished. The emotional effect on the viewer is exhausting—an appropriate feeling for one witnessing the rapid rise to power of a ruthless man. Yet the film is held together by counter forces—the repetition and overlapping of certain events and symbols in Kane's life as remembered by three different persons close to him. The repetitions help cement the illusion that this fabulous life really occurred, and the preview of it offered in the news documentary helps the viewer keep in mind the major lines of Kane's career even though the film moves constantly back and forth in time in relating it.

Historically, *Citizen Kane* was one of the first films to employ a number of devices now common in film making. It shows close-ups of faces along with sharply focused figures in the distance. It makes clear visually as much as verbally the psychological relationship of persons in the story. When the Italian voice coach stands gesturing angrily at Susan Alexander Kane as she flats her notes, Kane himself enters the room in the distance and stands authoritatively, waiting a second to size up the situation, then moving forward to tower over the voice coach even more commandingly than the coach towered over Susan.

The handling of dialogue is as bold and striking as the editing of the shots. Persons interrupt each other and several talk at once, for a few seconds preventing the viewer from hearing what is being said. Again, Welles risked confusing his viewers in order to suggest reality. In the mouths of the most intelligent and educated characters, the words spoken are more mature and sophisticated than viewers of the period were accustomed to hearing in motion pictures. For example, Jed Leland, Kane's left-hand man, in describing Kane to the reporter says, "He had a generous mind. I don't suppose anybody who ever lived had so many opinions . . . but he didn't believe in anything." The first statement sounds innocent, the second ironically turns the first to water, and the third is a further surprise. In speaking to Kane, Jed says, "You talk about the people as though you owned them . . . as if you made them a present of liberty as a reward for services rendered." Mr. Bernstein, Kane's right-hand man, speaks his simple admiration for his boss in boyish phrases totally unlike Jed's worldly-wise statements.

Like many long and complex works of art, this film has its weaknesses or inconsistencies. In several sequences Welles uses caricatures that seem inconsistent with his effort to create an unusual sense of reality. The deposed editor of the newspaper which Kane buys huffs and puffs like a frog as Kane takes over his office—acting like an exaggerated character from Dickens. The vaultlike library where the reporter hunts for the secret of "Rosebud" in a diary seems more a mausoleum than a private library. There the reporter is served by a mannish woman librarian and a womanish male guard. It is a nice touch to suggest the sterility of a misanthrope's private crypt of books but in picture and sound so exaggerated that it mars the tone of the film. The music in the film is too histrionic—almost humorous at times in its supercharging of a crescendo already fierce in the movement of shots one to another.

The power of a film director to bring forth the resources of his actors is illustrated in Welles' handling of Joseph Cotten, who plays his part on several levels with a subtlety that he has seldom if ever achieved in films directed by other men. Everett Sloane, playing Mr. Bernstein, captures a naïveté and childish enthusiasm which suggest a range of ability that has rarely been tapped in him since this film. In subsequent films and television dramas, he has consistently, albeit brilliantly, played a man of great power and sophistication.

Citizen Kane is not a film of beautiful shots that can be called "arty" rather than artistic. If its shots are occasionally beautiful, they are so for a purpose. When the aged Jed Leland sits in a wheelchair in a hospital corridor, the viewer is reminded of a painting by Honoré Daumier—the visored head, dark glasses, and white mustaches above the light dressing robe at the left of the frame, and in the distance two shadowy figures even less in the focus of the camera and of life than Jed, who lives only in memories as he talks to the reporter. A beautiful composition but one which holds its place in the larger sequence of shots and is saved from sentimentality by the jaunty and bitter commentary Jed speaks to the reporter and by the somewhat glaring, yet blurred light in which it is steeped.

The artistry of this film, particularly in its symbolism, may sometimes be unconscious on the part of the director. But like any competent work of art, this film has consistent movement and conception which show that its director was really directing it and suggest that even when he did not consciously construct a symbol or deeper meaning, he may have stumbled toward it because in a large way he knew where he was going.

For example, in the news documentary at the outset, the viewer sees Kane again and again through a barrier. He is behind a fence. People stand between him and the viewer. He is on the platform. He is inaccessible. The only times when we are really close to him are at the beginning when the snowing crystal ball paperweight falls from his hand and bounces crazily away from his feet.

The camera is looking down as if it sees through Kane's eyes in death. The snow falling within the paperweight repeats the snow just a moment before seen outside the window of Kane's room, and it flashes back to the snow in which Charles as a young boy was playing before he was taken from his parents to the big city. It is snowing outside Mr. Bernstein's office when he recalls to the reporter his memories of serving as Kane's general manager. The snow recalls something Charles used as a boy, which finally gives away the secret of Rosebud. The spectator reviews the public and contrived events of the life of an artificial man, back to the moment in boyhood when he was capable of feeling. Snow and Rosebud are the symbols of the warmth of meaning which his adult life so lacked. There is no barrier between Kane and himself and Kane and the viewer at those moments.

The film opens and closes on the sign at the entrance to Xanadu: NO TRESPASSING. *Citizen Kane* shows the kaleidoscopic life of a man of empty importance who bought people but did not know them. No trespassing on this life, but the ironies are all there, for the camera has trespassed and revealed the man. He is not the hero of a Greek tragedy who comes finally to insight out of blindness. Others see him, but he never sees himself. He is drugged with egomania. Except for his moments of nostalgia (in boyhood before corruption), he betrays only a few seconds of boyish good humor with a girl or with journalistic colleagues, who admire him naïvely or see him with grudging disillusion. How much of this continuity of feeling and idea was consciously created by Director Orson Welles we cannot know. But it is not all luck that so much of it is there.

To analyze this work, or any film, completely, one would have to consider at least some of the following questions, many of which have not been answered here:

1. What is the order of the conscious stream of sequences? What is their relationship to one another? How do we get from one sequence to another?
2. Are the individual shots visually authentic? In what way are they significant?
3. Are the pictures trite or fresh? Conventionally or uniquely composed?
4. What sound effects are employed? With what purpose?
5. Do the actors draw believable characterizations? What particular gestures or mannerisms are employed to suggest characterization?
6. From whose point or points of view is the story told?
7. What ironies are present, in visual sequence, dialogue, or event?
8. What objects, statements, or events become symbolic? How?

9. Of what importance is the dialogue? What varieties and levels of language are present?
10. Is the story contrived, melodramatic, or inevitable? Does the outcome depend upon chance or does it grow logically out of the impact of character upon character and of event upon character?
11. What moral attitudes are revealed by characters within the action or by the writer or director?
12. What mythical elements are present?
13. In what sense is the picture "true" to life? Are the people portrayed simple or complex? What reaction is expected from the audience; are we to sympathize, to be horrified, to hate, or to laugh?
14. What values does the picture as a complete experience seem to recognize and support?

One cannot remember and criticize a film as he does a linear composition like a short story or novel, and perhaps the attempt to do so is dangerous. A film cannot be stopped and remain a moving picture. The method of analysis used here is probably the least frustrating: to take notes (on several viewings of a film) of those shots and sequences which strike one most powerfully and then to generalize upon those examples which seem to group themselves as recurring principles or techniques. Giving the students one such analysis of a complete film will help them see the complexity of motion pictures. They should not be given such analysis again and again, or the teacher may rob them of their eyes and the pleasure of seeing a film as if for the first time. To take away from a film its impact of newness and instantaneousness is to paralyze it as a medium.

CHAPTER SEVEN

Structure
of a Film

NOVEL VERSUS FILM

In order to ask whether the picture adapted from a novel
has remained faithful to the spirit of the novel, we must look
for thematic similarities. Novels which are thematically similar
may yet have marked structural differences. A motion picture
and the novel from which it has been adapted can be assumed
to have thematic links. Their structures, however, will be different, and inasmuch as theme is never perceived independ-
ently of form, film content must be assessed not against the
content or structure of the related novel but within the form of
the film itself.

THE GRAPES OF WRATH: NOVEL AND FILM

John Steinbeck's novel *The Grapes of Wrath* was published in 1939. In 1940 Darryl Zanuck produced a motion picture based on Steinbeck's novel, scripted by Nunnally Johnson
and directed by John Ford. The film received critical approval; the literary critic Edmund Wilson noted the cinematic
quality of Steinbeck's novel, ". . . *The Grapes of Wrath* went
on the screen as easily as if it had been written in the studios."
However, careful study of the novel and film reveals significant
differences as well as startling similarities.

Steinbeck's novel has thirty chapters. Nearly a third of
these are interchapters, usually, less than five pages in length,
interrupting the plot continuity but carrying a heavy load of

meaning. Some are symbolic; others are socioeconomic-political and allow Steinbeck to comment on the implications of the plot. In most of these interchapters, the writing tends to shift from Steinbeck's pictorial and descriptive style to more generalized observation. Since films are less capable of generalizing than novels, it is not surprising to find the content of the interchapters almost entirely absent from the film.

THE INTERCHAPTERS OF *THE GRAPES OF WRATH*

Chapter Three of the novel is highly symbolic. We find a land turtle "dragging his high-domed shell over the grass." He claws his way up an embankment; he hurries across the burning heat of the highway. One driver swerves to avoid hitting the turtle; another swerves toward it, deliberately. The turtle is spun off the highway but pulls itself erect. Rugged, undaunted, yellow toes slipping a fraction in the dust, it moves forward remorselessly.

The land turtle, like the Joads, is indomitable. Harried by some, avoided by others, the turtle continues to survive. It symbolically foreshadows the plight of the Okies as they claw their way across a continent. But this brief incident, significant and powerful in the novel, does not serve the film director's purposes. Instead, early shots in the film suggest the awesome power of nature. Man and his dusty environment are contrasted by means of spatial editing. We see Tom Joad and Jim Casy walking across the eroded dustbowl countryside. They are antlike in size against the wind, sky, and horizon.

Chapter Seven of the novel breaks the forward movement and serves as a commentary on it. Steinbeck describes a used-car lot, its predatory personnel ready to destroy the victims of drought, dust, and land companies. "Owners with rolled-up sleeves. Salesmen, neat, deadly, small intent eyes watching for weaknesses." Again, the chapter is capable of larger extension; these are the ravenous exploiting the distressed. These are the vicious and dishonest, fattening on the friendless and unfortunate. They are harbingers of the injustices to be encountered along the road and repeated in California. Here is the cruel reality foreshadowing the wrath ahead.

Chapter Nine intensifies the unrelenting pressures on the farmers forced off their land. Steinbeck describes their anguish as they sell their implements and possessions, laden with memories, for a fractional part of their worth. A plow sells for four dollars; a team of bays and wagon go for ten. With a mixture of anger and compassion, Steinbeck links the bitter present to a less brutal past.

> Ten dollars? For both? And the wagon—Oh, Jesus Christ! I'd shoot 'em for dog feed first. Oh, take 'em! Take 'em quick, mister, you're buying a little girl plaiting the forelocks, taking off her hair ribbon to make bows, standing back, head cocked, rubbing the soft noses with her cheek. You're buying years of work, toil in the sun; you're buying a sorrow that can't talk.

In a later paragraph Steinbeck adds, "How can we live without our lives? How will we know it's us without our past? No. Leave it. Burn it." John Ford, directing the motion picture, selected one effective visual sequence to symbolize the uprooting of the farm families. The camera comes up close as Ma Joad agonizes over a series of items—each bearing its sentimental associations. Item by item is discarded or burned. Steinbeck's words are turned into haunting visual images. The camera focuses on Ma Joad in a searching close-up as the fire consumes her keepsakes.

In Chapter Eleven Steinbeck writes coldly and tersely about the land after the farmers are gone. He describes the mechanical work of the bulldozers—unemotional, uncaring. He shifts to the deserted houses now occupied by mice, owls, and bats. The symbolic fauna, less than human, share in the deposition of families. Without human beings about, nature becomes even more destructive. The mewing cats are now hunting cats. Weeds spring up. The smell of bat droppings permeates the ragged houses. But this two and a half page interchapter—while highly concrete and therefore visual—does not appear in the film. In the novel its symbolic conceptual purpose is clear. But the great power of the short chapter is verbal and symbolic. It functions as another commentary on the realities afflicting the farmers.

Chapter Fourteen is political and abstract. Steinbeck describes the symbolic change from "I" to "we." He implies the tremendous political power that can explode when exploited people share their griefs and then their strength. Steinbeck links Paine, Marx, Jefferson, and Lenin. The ideas in the chapter are conceptual and verbal, not visual.

John Ford recognizes Steinbeck's "we" motif. Ma Joad speaks the hopeful lines taken from Chapter Twenty, ". . . we're the people that live. They ain't gonna wipe us out. Why, we're the people—we go on." The speech comes at the *end* of the film—but only *two-thirds* through the novel. When we compare the overall structure of the film and novel, the pattern used by John Ford in his adaptation will be made clearer.

Chapter Twenty-one is only three pages long. But its content would require a series of films to particularize. Steinbeck piles concept on concept. He describes the hostility encountered by the migrants, an hostility welding the Okies together. He understands the fears that produce local cruelties. With compassion he portrays the exploitation of migrants willing to work for below subsistence wages. He concludes with a political-economic observation, ". . . money that might have gone to wages went for gas, for guns . . . On the highways the people moved like ants and searched for work, for food. And the anger began to ferment." The chapter deals, not with the Joads, or the Wilsons, or the Littlefields, or the Bullitts but with the "moving questing people." John Ford catches the spirit of the chapter when he accompanies Ma Joad's "We're the people" with a dissolve to more and more trucks moving out onto the highways. The migrants, restless, uprooted people, have begun to move. And the fermenting anger is captured in visual patterns.

Chapter Twenty-five contains a powerful indictment, one that would necessitate extensive film footage to document visually. Steinbeck conjures up a contrast between the know-how which produces fertile fields and the economic system that mocks man's humanity. A compact verbal illustration sums up the concept. "And children dying of pellagra must die because a profit cannot be taken from an orange." Steinbeck contrasts hungry people and kerosene-sprayed, dumped oranges. The fermenting discontent of an earlier interchapter yields the wine of rage.

In Chapter Twenty-seven Steinbeck's rage burns steadily. He describes the plight of the migrant workers, cheated by crooked scales and company stores, defeated by their own needy numbers, lured to California by misleading handbills issued by unscrupulous landowners. In Chapter Twenty-nine work becomes nonexistent. Steinbeck parallels his narrative of the Joads with the story of migrant people in general.

Women watch their men fearfully; can a man sustain his spirit under repeated indignities? But the break never comes; fear turns to anger, not despair. Steinbeck concludes his last interchapter on the pale green hope of spring, a curious hope foreshadowing the ambivalence of his closing chapter. Rose of Sharon's child dies, stillborn. But her last symbolic biological act, nursing the dying farmer, completes the "we" of an earlier interchapter. Rose of Sharon and the gaunt farmer symbolize the unquenchable human spirit.

Out of these nine interchapters John Ford filmed a single sequence. It is interesting to note that the narrative affecting the Joads received much more attention than the more abstract shorter chapters. Yet, even in the deletions from the remaining two-thirds of the novel, certain patterns persist.

THEME AND STRUCTURE IN *THE GRAPES OF WRATH*

Edmund Wilson perceives a "substratum which remains constant" in *The Grapes of Wrath*—Steinbeck's "preoccupation with biology." [1] *The Grapes of Wrath* teems with flora and fauna ranging from spearhead seeds to carloads of oranges, from vermin to mules. Animal metaphor fills the novel both in descriptions and dialogue. Some of the dialogue is retained in the film; most of the small fauna disappear. Instead, the visual imagery pits man against the enormity of nature. Many of the early shots portray human characters dwarfed by the environment.

In the film the potentially objectionable language of the novel disappears, as well as much dialogue. Not only are the swear words omitted but so are most of the irreverent terms. Ma Joad's fierce resentment of the religious zealots and their seething hell-fire disappears. Casy's natural morality with its mockery of his early evangelism also disappears. The obvious similarities between the Casy who has ceased being a preacher and Casy as Christ are not emphasized. The creators of the film decided that the irony of a man's becoming more Christlike by foregoing formal religion is too sensitive a subject for the film to concentrate upon. Instead, we watch Casy's natural morality operating in approved sociological channels. The political-economic villains of Steinbeck's novel become more general in the film. The deputies and sheriffs who provoke Ma Joad to near violence are not clearly symbolic of identifiable groups in the film, although they represent the landowners and local

[1] Edmund Wilson, *The Boys in the Back Room* (Colt, 1941), p. 61.
George Bluestone, *Novels into Film* (Berkeley, University of California Press, 1961), p. 147.

political leaders in the novel. Perhaps most significant of all, the film ends on a note of optimism as Ma Joad declares hopefully, "We're the people. . . ." But the social and economic problems have not been solved; the film provides an apparent solution without actually coming to grips with the real difficulties.

As the picture opens, while the credits are still flashing across the screen, we hear "Red River Valley," folk music, a bittersweet leitmotif, authentic and moving. In the scene when Ma relinquishes her keepsakes to the flames—the truck is already piled dangerously high—we hear the refrain again while we watch Ma's unspoken anguish tempered by a fierce courage. In the closing scene of Ma's paean, we hear, once more, the sad-hopeful melody. Indeed, this closing scene appeals in many ways. It dissolves to the visual symbol of trucks swarming onto the highways heading West. The implication is clear; Ma's observation is warranted by the natural unbreaking human spirit, which moves like a powerful tide.

Absolute silence accompanies some visual details. The Joads silently face their evictors; Ma looks at her earrings in a mirror; signs signifying the vastness of distance; place names to be conquered shortly, all call for silence or near-silence. Silhouettes of Tom Joad and Jim Casy against the light sky, the wind blowing the dust and clouds across the plains, the faces of migrants after listening to a man debunking the illusions suggested by handbills promising work for all, these are dramatic shots and sequences. So are the close-ups of Muley, Grandpa refusing to leave, Grandma spooning in food, Casy unsuccessfully leaping a fence, Tom's leave-taking of Ma Joad, the mountain of tin cans, the silence of migrant children watching for food, the almost unbelieving looks on the faces of human beings when the government camp administrator speaks some simple friendly words. When Muley tells of the tractors pushing people off their land, his eyes take on a haunted, wild look. He says, "A man come one day . . . ," and his voice continues while a dissolve brings in the scene with fearful immediacy. After a few seconds, the camera returns to Muley in a close-up as he remembers, "They come with the cats. . . ." And, once again, we see the caterpillar push over Muley's house, and it almost seems to lame the man himself. Adding to the utter frustration are the few questions and answers preceding the sequence. Muley can't find out who's to blame; there's no villainous individual opposing him. Instead, there's a land company and behind that a bank, and on it goes, becoming less human at each remove.

When the Joads leave for California, the last we see of their home is the wind blowing open the clattering door and the whirling of dust. Silhouette shots continue. We see the truck against the flat sky; we watch place names and road signs. No oral comment is added to a particularly symbolic sign—"water 15¢ gallon."

In the novel Ma Joad symbolizes the fierce determination to keep the family unit intact. As long as there is family unity, there is hope. Tom's departure is a loss beyond repair. Tom Joad symbolizes—and verbalizes—the necessity for human dignity. His statement is retained in the film. Protesting the indignities suffered by the migrant people, Tom says of the deputies, ". . . if it was the law . . . why, we could take it. But it ain't the law. . . . They're workin' away at our spirits. . . . They're workin' on our decency."

Both Muley and Grandpa symbolize an attachment to the land. Muley will die on the land; Grandpa died when they took his away. In an interchapter Steinbeck describes a tractor driver as ". . . driving a dead tractor on land he does not know and love. . . ."

One key speech in the novel suggests the significance of Casy's complex role. He is asked to say a grace; he begins by noting his own confusions, and Jesus' confusions before going off into the wilderness. Casy says,

I ain't saying I'm like Jesus. . . . But I got tired like Him, an' I got mixed up like Him, an' I went into the wilderness like Him . . . Sometimes I'd pray like I always done. On'y I couldn't figure what I was prayin' to or for. There was the hills, an' there was me, an' we wasn't separate no more. We was one thing. An' that one thing was holy.

The large themes—the unity of family, love of land, the necessity of human dignity—are retained by John Ford. These themes include religious hypocrisy, political and economic misuses of power, and their implications. The sociological injustices that batter the migrants take the form of powerful visual indictments, general rather than explicit.

A significant structural pattern in the novel is modified in the film. While Chapters Twenty-three, Twenty-five, Twenty-six, Twenty-seven, Twenty-eight, Twenty-nine, and Thirty of the novel portray Tom's forced flight, Casy's death, the exploitation of the migrant workers, intolerable abuses to the human spirit and the oncoming of greater violence, the film closes on the government camp sequences—the most optimistic moments in the novel. Even Tom's farewell seems less disruptive in the context of the government camp setting. The novel's thirty chapters are a radically different structure from that of the film. But the wrath which the interchapters communicate to the reader is generated in the film by the film's structure of shots and sequences, which replace the interchapters.

John Ford's film, like any worthwhile novel, rewards close examination. Its characters, themes, symbols, structure, shot sequence, spatial editing, and sound effects add up to a complex work of art. The pictorial writing of a John Steinbeck results in powerful film images. The structure and editing by the film director and script writer establish the context for the individual shots and sequences. The role of the viewer is first to respond, then achieve a sense of detachment, and finally to assess the artistic merit of the film—its form and meaning.

CHAPTER EIGHT

Imaginary
Gardens

> Art, broadly, is the form of life or the sound or color of life.
> Considered as form (in the abstract) it is often indistinguish-
> able from life itself.[1]

Some movies have always been made which are true to life.
They not only find wide audiences but also succeed in exciting
the kind of serious critical attention rarely devoted to mass
media.

In art, being true to life is not a matter of reflecting man's
daily routine. Life itself, as has been noted earlier in this book,
is chaotic and meaningless until the mind imposes some order
upon it. Art, of course, is a part of life. Its validity depends
upon the degree of order and structure, the genuineness of the
relationship between its elements, its faithfulness to a form, in
essence, its sincerity, not reproduction of life. Its importance
depends upon the subject matter and whether there is any
degree of high seriousness about it. Its success depends on the
degree to which the spectator can recognize in it universal
truth. The world of Hamlet's Elsinore is fantastic in terms of
our own, from which we have long since succeeded in eliminating ghosts. The play survives because in its complex structure we see all mankind crawling between earth and heaven.
There is a little Hamlet in us all.

Not everyone can read *Hamlet,* and not every play can
attempt to be *Hamlet.* Nor do we expect all manifestations of

[1] Wallace Stevens, "Adagia," *Opus Posthumous* (New York, Knopf,
1957).

112

any medium to possess the excellence to make it survive. We *can* expect of any art form, and the more so of any highly effective art form like the movie, that it withstand critical examination in terms of its form, its theme, its parts, and its structure.

The creation of mass media for a large audience usually results in a leveling downward of quality in order to attempt to satisfy that audience. Such a situation existed too, from the beginning, with drama. But there has been no truly great drama that did not reach a heterogeneous audience. And the same has been true of films. The attempt to satisfy a large audience of heterogeneous tastes and biases has resulted, not entirely inadvertently, in some kinds of excellence. Three genres in particular demonstrate the kind of refinement possible when the industry develops its products to perfection.

First of these is the documentary. By definition such a film attempts to make some point about real life and support its contention with convincing evidence. Some documentaries have become among the most famous and most respected of all movies. A documentary like *Nanook of the North* (1922), actually the unpretentious story of an Eskimo family's fight for food, succeeded because the director, Robert Flaherty, was highly selective in his choice of detail and sequence. Ranging from the travelogue or newsreel at one extreme and the highly sophisticated indoctrination of the United States Army's *Why We Fight Series* at the other, the documentary brings concreteness, vividness, and excitement to the study of places and events.

A second genre is the elaborate musical comedy. As it developed on the American stage, it became itself a unique American production. Indebted originally to the opera and the operetta as they evolved in Europe, the American counterpart attained a respectable status when music, lyric, dialogue, and choreography were carefully related to one another; each functioned as an integral and necessary part of the whole.

It was entirely natural that Hollywood would present musical comedies. The nature of the medium itself gave an added richness to the result, so that choreography became multidimensional, color and costume more lavish, and the musical score embellished and intensified. While Hollywood was capable of making what were probably embroidered copies of successful Broadway productions, it was also capable of showing varying degrees of respect for the peculiar conventions of the genre which can survive the translation of dimension and time.

For every lavish and uninspired *South Pacific* there has been a compensating *The Music Man,* which preserves the grace and bounce of the stage version but enlarges the sense of fantasy so in keeping with the spirit of the comedy that it becomes not so much a period piece as a myth. Professor Harold Hill is portrayed as a picaresque Pied Piper, and the movie becomes a timeless statement of the power of the imagination to transform the narrow routine of living into something magical and colorful. As the vision of the girl at the close transforms the tawdry and ill-fitting uniforms of Harold Hill's motley band into spectacular costumes, so do the color camera and the energy of Director Morton da Costa transform the original play into a cinematic fairy tale.

A third genre indigenous to this country is the western, a form which perpetuates and refines a preoccupation with American frontier life until the form itself is not history but art. Bret Harte, Mark Twain, and Owen Wister were among those responsible for its early forms in literature. In the movies the form probably began with Edwin Porter's *The Great Train Robbery* (1903), and includes Victor Fleming's filming of Wister's *The Virginian,* with Gary Cooper and Walter Huston —two stars whose personal careers are inextricably intertwined with the development of the western itself.[2]

[2] Characters in westerns, as well as in other movies, have been accepted as part of the folklore of American culture. James Reston, for example, commenting on the death of President Kennedy, referred to his sheer verve and joy, imparting youth, in contrast to President Johnson's appeal. Mr. Reston

The West in the American western is almost entirely a mythical place, existing in the imagination as in the legend. But westerns have their own truth and their own excellence. The most successful have been the result of the refinement of a pattern in existence since *The Virginian* but so adapted to the film medium that, like Fred Zinnemann's *High Noon,* starring Gary Cooper, they are almost perfect artistically. They have been faithful to their own conventions: good and evil personified in the characters of the marshal, or gunfighter, and the bad men; the showdown at the end and the concretized and immediate dramatization of the conflict between good and evil; the bare, windswept western town, the economical embodiment of Everyman's meager lot.

According to Robert Warshow, "The Westerner is the last gentleman, and the movies which over and over again tell his story are probably the last art form in which the concept of honor retains its strength." [3]

There may be no Wild West or River City, Iowa, but if a movie is honest and true to its form it can accomplish what Marianne Moore claimed for poetry and "present for inspection, 'imaginary gardens with real toads in them.' " [4]

The freedom for film makers to be true to life, whether in a realistic or mythical way, has always been under attack, for the movie reaches a wide and varied audience, including young children. In 1915, the United States Supreme Court ruled that "The exhibition of moving pictures is a business,

---

assumed that readers would understand the allusion to *High Noon* in his quotation from a correspondent to his column in the New York *Times:*

"Mr. Johnson now seems Gary Cooper as President—*High Noon,* the poker game, the easy walk and masculine smile. But even Gary Cooper was growing older, and the companions and adversaries around the poker table reflect a less fresh, if no doubt practical and effective mood. All will be well, I feel sure, but it is August, not June. . . ."

Friday, December 13, 1963

[3] Robert Warshow, "American Movies," *The Immediate Experience* (Garden City, Doubleday, Anchor, 1962), p. 141.

[4] Marianne Moore, "Poetry," *Collected Poems* (New York, Macmillan, 1951), p. 41.

pure and simple, originated and conducted for profit, like other spectacles, not to be regarded, nor intended to be regarded . . . as a part of the press of the country or as organs of public opinion." This decision, made in response to the challenge of a distributor in Ohio, resulted in the acceptance of film censorship until the decision of May 26, 1952.

By 1922 when public opinion had been aroused and censorship bills were before thirty-two state legislatures, industry leaders formed their own organization for public relations and the protection of the industry. Will Hays, Postmaster General of the United States at the time, became chairman of the organization called the Motion Picture Producers and Distributors of America (MPPDA). The so-called "Hays Code," recommended to that group by Mr. Hays, was adopted in 1930. The "code of morals" had been drawn up by a trade paper publisher and a Roman Catholic priest. It provided arbitrary restraint.

After the Legion of Decency was established by the Roman Catholic Church in 1933, the industry set up a Production Code Administration to read film scripts, identify what it considered undesirable elements and then register approval with what came to be known as the "seal." Although the Administration was self-regulating and had no legal control over producers or distributors or indvidual theatre owners, it could bring pressures to bear on the makers of movies to guarantee a "high moral tone" in each movie.

The Production Code was established by a society that had its roots in Puritanism and by an industry genuinely concerned with the quality of its films. It was one of several mechanisms devoted to guarding the public morals by passing judgment on moving pictures even before they were made. Others were the various groups of state and local censoring boards, operating with the implicit sanction of the Supreme Court decision of 1915 and devoted specifically to prohibiting the showing of those pictures which the individuals who composed the boards considered not to be in the public interest.

The Code tended to strengthen and perpetuate the wish that certain elemental impulses in the human being did not exist; it restricted the subject matter of the movies either to bland domestic comedy or forced them to conceal more elemental material behind the religious, the historical, or the documentary. In general, the Code attempted to regulate and in many cases prohibit presentations of sex, religion, the use of drugs or liquor, and to eliminate such scenes of the ultimate act of murder as stabbing, blows on the head, the sight of a man being struck by a bullet at close range.

The Code was based on the assumption that art can be morally evil as well as morally good. It cites as the first of its Reasons Underlying Particular Applications, *"Sin and evil enter into the story of human beings and hence in themselves are valid dramatic material."* [5]

It goes on to say: "In the use of this material, it must be distinguished between *sin which repels* by its very nature, and *sins which often attract,"* and it goes on to define further.

The fact that sin and evil (and their corollary, suffering) exist in the world is not only self-evident but so inherent in the human condition that there is no valid dramatic material in which evil is not in some way imbedded. Granted that the overwhelming reality of the moving picture form brings us closer to the events it portrays; nevertheless, it is difficult to prove that these events cause a behavioral change any greater than that caused by the events described in novels, plays, or other art forms. That the Codes have often fulfilled a useful function is fairly obvious. They help to establish criteria for maintaining levels of decency, recognizing the responsibility of the mass media to its audiences, and establishing a degree of

[5] Robert C. O'Hara, *Media for the Millions* (New York, Random House, 1961), p. 381.

order, recognizing the responsibility of the artist to his material.

In defense of the Code it must be pointed out that a large number of thoroughly satisfying and honest pictures were made during the many years of its existence. Among them were *All Quiet on the Western Front, Anna Christie* (1930); *Street Scene* (1931); *A Farewell to Arms* (1932); *The Informer* (1935); *Dodsworth* (1936); *The Life of Emile Zola, The Good Earth* (1937); *Pygmalion* (1938); *Gone with the Wind, Goodby, Mr. Chips, Stagecoach* (1939); *The Grapes of Wrath, Our Town* (1940); *Citizen Kane, How Green Was My Valley* (1941); *For Whom the Bell Tolls, Madame Curie, The Ox-Bow Incident* (1943); *The Corn Is Green, A Bell for Adano* (1945); *The Treasure of Sierra Madre* (1948); *Pinky, The Heiress, All the King's Men* (1949); *Cyrano de Bergerac* (1950); *A Streetcar Named Desire, The Red Badge of Courage, The African Queen* (1951); *High Noon* (1952); *The Cruel Sea, From Here to Eternity* (1953); and *On the Waterfront, The Caine Mutiny* (1954).[6]

During the same years the general cultural and moral climate of the country was changing, and the Code tended to reflect that climate, although always conservatively. The taste in the country during the war years, for example, ran to the light-hearted and escapist themes or to the chauvinistic. After the war, this country like the rest of the world was gradually subjected to vast changes in attitudes and taste, reflected first in the postwar literature in France, England, and this country as well. Ultimately the movies also approached themes they had hitherto avoided; both producers and audience recognized an increase in sophistication and growing awareness of the psychological complexities of life.

At the time when television was capturing a great part of the mass audience that had previously attended films, European films gradually found an audience in this country, enthu-

[6] Daniel Blum, *A Pictorial History of the Talkies* (New York, Putnam's, 1958), pp. 21-277.

siastic and demanding, ready for the realism of postwar European artists. Subjects which the American industry had avoided now found a public ready to leave its television sets as well as to miss the play at the local theatre in order to see, in small art theatres or in film societies, such foreign pictures as Rossellini's *Open City,* de Sica's *The Bicycle Thief,* Kurosawa's *Rashomon,* Truffaut's *The Four Hundred Blows,* and Bergman's *Wild Strawberries.*

In 1952, the power of certain state and private organizations to censor films was weakened by Supreme Court decisions, when the Court ruled that Rossellini's *The Miracle* could not be banned in New York on the grounds of sacrilege; nor could *Pinky* be banned in southern sections of the country on the grounds of racial controversy. The Court also proclaimed, in a belated step, "that motion pictures are a medium of communication and are entitled to the constitutional guarantees of free speech and free press under the First and Fourteenth Amendments." [7] In the meantime, the Code has been so revised that its emphasis is more and more on the treatment of the subject than on the subject itself. Today there are few subjects that may not be touched upon.[8]

The influx of foreign films and the lessening of the powers of censorship by public or private means has increased attendance. Although there are now fewer movie houses by one-third than there were after the close of World War II, there is evidence that the fall off in attendance has been reversed and that movie going has been gradually becoming more popular as a pastime.

Part of the increase may be due to the phenomenon of the drive-in movie, which appeals to an audience of teenagers and youths in their early twenties, as well as to parents who can bring children in the car. While of considerable significance to

[7] Bosley Crowther, *Movies and Censorship.* Public Affairs Pamphlet, No. 332 (New York, Public Affairs Committee, 1962), pp. 9-20.

[8] Arthur Mayer, "How Much Can the Movies Say?" *Saturday Review,* November 3, 1962, pp. 18-20, 52-53.

the sociologist, the relationship between behavior at a drive-in and the quality of the movie is difficult even to speculate on.

Part of the increase is due to a more sophisticated audience responding to pictures dealing with subjects once considered too dangerous, such as drug addiction and homosexuality. The emancipation from earlier restrictions has resulted in pictures whose ultimate merit may be questionable, no matter how great the entertainment value. Billy Wilder's *The Apartment,* for example, hilarious as it is, seems to take place in an utter moral vacuum, presenting as a social phenomenon the late afternoon assignation without taking any moral attitude toward it. But other pictures have tackled controversial subjects honestly and powerfully. Otto Preminger's *The Man with the Golden Arm* attacked the problem of drug addiction head-on.

It is difficult to say whether the popularity of the foreign film is due to a reaction against the American film or to some virtue inherent in the imported one. The foreign film may have some appeal to Americans merely because it comes from a foreign country. American films have long had a lucrative following abroad; over half the income from our own movies is made from overseas showing.

Imported films, especially those which are the result of the wave of Italian Neorealism, deal more bluntly with actuality than do most of our own. As an immediate consequence they are likely to present subjects that are more sensational or controversial; the Japanese *Rashomon* seeks to find the truth among four conflicting accounts of adultery and murder. Tony Richardson's *A Taste of Honey* from a British play is the story of an unwed mother, with a homosexual in a strong supporting role. Rossellini's *Two Women* is a blunt, jolting, and compassionate account of the raping of a mother and her daughter in wartime. Delbert Mann's *The Mark* explores the painful convalescence of a man convicted of a sexual aberration.

By its nature sex provides highly dramatic material, and

hence the frank treatment of it has been the chief ingredient in many an Italian and French film. Even now in many American films, the direction and the writing seem to suffer from a kind of evasion which may be a carryover from the old days. Billy Wilder's *Irma La Douce* is a wildly comic film, and some of the acting is first-rate, but its initial assumption and continued assertion that prostitution is fun is not satiric enough to reconcile the viewer to the truth of the situation. The picture is specious and deeply immoral because so untrue to life.

The existence of the ordinary man, caught in the struggle of making a living and providing for his children, has supplied material for the outstanding French comedies like *The Baker's Wife* and *The Well-Digger's Daughter* and for the major Italian directors like de Sica. His *The Bicycle Thief* presents an ordinary lower class workman whose one desire is a job and to whom the theft of his bicycle, his only means of transportation, is a catastrophe of significance.

As both foreign and American films present more and more direct views of life in all its aspects, parents must decide what to say about their children's seeing these films. An uninhibited range of subjects has always been dealt with in literature. Now they are being presented with increasing frankness and graphic abruptness in films like *Victim, The Children's Hour, The Man with the Golden Arm, Lolita, The Mark, Walk on the Wild Side,* and *Splendor in the Grass,* which appear in neighborhood theatres for a large and heterogeneous audience. In "A Dilemma for the Family," Peter Bunzel says:

> The fact is that these movies [of this kind] are not intended for children. They are, by and large, thoughtful films for grownups—all made with the box office in mind, but rarely crassly commercial. Most are adapted from distinguished books and plays. They deal with major, serious social problems. Yet children will see some of them. They will hear discussions about them and read about them . . . the films present a dilemma to be solved within the family and unless

the problems are openly discussed at an adult level they cannot be intelligently and honestly met.[9]

At the same time a trend in film making presents a problem, as Hollis Alpert suggests:

> This trend of the industry, bucked only by an occasional release from the Disney studios, unfortunately signifies less a growing maturity on the part of our film makers than an increased predilection for pseudosophisticated dialogue and risqué situations within a conventional frame.[10]

The worst thing that adults can do is to pretend that such films, and hence such issues, do not exist. To prevent young people who may constitute a major portion of the audience from seeing such films is difficult if not impossible. The suggestion that such material is "bad" for the teenager is probably sufficient in itself to guarantee attendance. To resuscitate or create new censorship agencies will not only renew the evasive abuses which resulted from meeting the terms of the original Production Code but will perpetuate a far more serious error: to remove from the growing individual the necessity and possibility of facing choice.

And herein lies a primary concern of educators. Several centuries ago, the author of *Paradise Lost* wrote:

> Good and evill we know in the field of this World grow up together almost inseparably; and the knowledge of good is so involv'd and interwoven with the knowledge of evil, and in so many cunning resemblances hardly to be discern'd, that those confused seeds which were impos'd on *Psyche* as an incessant labour to cull out, and sort asunder, were not more intermixt. It was from out the rinde of one apple tasted, that

---

[9] Peter Bunzel, "A Dilemma for the Family," *Life* Magazine, February 23, 1962, pp. 88-89.

[10] Hollis Alpert, "Women and Children First," *Saturday Review*, November 16, 1963, p. 29.

the knowledge of good and evill as two twins cleaving together leapt forth into the World. And perhaps this is that doom which *Adam* fell into of knowing good and evill, that is to say of knowing good by evill.[11]

Milton continues in his *Areopagitica,* an essay arguing against state censorship of books in 1644, to point out that little credit is due that person who, never having had to choose, succeeds in forbearing:

> I cannot praise a fugitive and cloister'd vertue, unexercis'd & unbreath'd, that never sallies out and seeks her adversary, but slinks out of the race, where that immortall garland is to be run for, not without dust and heat.[12]

Movies as they are being produced are adding to an international body of an acknowledged and important art form whose social, moral, and aesthetic implications need to be recognized and understood. It will be necessary to provide the emerging audience for these films with sensible criteria by which to understand, interpret, and judge the values of these films. Except for courses in film appreciation which can be and are being taught at the university level [13] and sporadically in secondary schools, it will remain largely up to the English teacher as well as the parents to bring attention to the necessary criteria.

Open discussion within the family, with adults, has always helped young people to gain understanding of the adult world. The moving picture treats sometimes the most violent aspects of that world, as well as the continuing conflict of adolescents with that world. Sometimes discussion within the classroom

---

[11] Frank Allen Patterson (ed.), *The Works of John Milton.* Vol. IV, (New York, Columbia, 1931), pp. 310-311.

[12] *Ibid.,* p. 311.

[13] *Motion Picture Production Facilities of Selected Colleges and Universities.* U.S. Department of Health, Education, and Welfare (Washington, U.S. Government Printing Office, 1963).

may help, although certain films are going to raise problems so delicate that discussion in a mixed class of teenagers would be impossible for all but the most adroit teacher. Whether discussed within the classroom or in the home, however, these movies are going to need the same critical appraisal that is normally leveled at music, literature, or any other art form whose subject matter is dramatic.

It is not the subject matter in isolation that determines which picture will be praised or condemned but the honesty and taste with which the film approaches the problem. It is not the subject matter, but the totality of the picture—genre, structure, order, detail, the relationship of the part to the whole, the technique, the color, and the sound, as well as tone and attitude—which must be considered, as form, in an evaluation of the quality of the moving picture.

Yet no one will deny that the new candor of the American movie presents problems simply because of the subject matter. Vicarious experiences from the movies offer many wise, healthy lessons which if experienced directly may be disastrous. The question of regulation is a complex and delicate one, and parents and educators are caught between attempting to protect youth against the shocking in human nature, on the one hand, and attempting to maintain a philosophical position which includes the right of free speech, the free exploration of ideas, and the right of freedom of choice on the other.

The answer may be some form of classification, as is often carried out by well-motivated agencies for the censoring of films, so that the public is informed by a responsible group of educators or publishers whether a film is suitable for a particular group. Such dividing lines are arbitrary; some sixteen-year-olds are already adults, and some will never be. In addition, some advertisers will probably never resist the temptation to exploit the classification in order to attract the prurient. The *Green Sheet,* a monthly survey of current films by representatives of ten national organizations, has five audience symbols:

adults, A; mature young people, MT; young people, Y; general audience, GA; and children (unaccompanied by Adults), C.[14]

The interactions between a society and its manifestations in popular art are incredibly complex. Yet these manifestations involve the responsible English teacher, who will find perennial themes of human experience in all societies in mass media as well as in literature and will be concerned with the treatment of those themes in the mass media art forms.

The rejoinder will be made that there are already problems enough in the selection of books for classroom study without taking on the more delicate one of discussing movies. Yet books of all kinds are readily available in drug stores and libraries, from the cheap and lurid to the substantial and serious, and the subject matter for the one is likely to be much like the subject matter for the other. We cannot evade the responsibility for dealing with a *Peyton Place,* should that unfortunate occasion arise, any more than we would refrain from examining *Antony and Cleopatra,* simply because each work presents sexual experience. Nor can we ignore the fact that students are also seeing movies of all sorts, with less supervision and with far less critical and wholesome discussion. To what extent does the willing spectator, like the central character in Walker Percy's *The Moviegoer* (Knopf, 1962), model his life after the world created for him by the movie maker?

When the occasion arises, then, it is the responsibility of the English teacher to furnish the student with the means of developing a dependable critical taste, to arm him against the shoddy, the tasteless, and the ephemeral and hopefully and ideally to make him a better human being. The teacher's concern and the student's is eventually to examine the human condition and sustain the belief that that condition is a dignified and noble one.

What questions can we teach a student to ask in his exam-

[14] Film Estimate Board of National Organizations, 522 Fifth Avenue, New York, New York 10036.

ination of a current motion picture? How can he measure it and increase his perception at the same time? In many cases the questions will be the same that are leveled at a work of literature. They will seek to discover the depth and the insight into characterization. They will probe the motivations of the various characters. They will analyze the validity and honesty of the setting. They will reveal whether the accumulation of incident and the eventual outcome are reasonable and stem from the effect of character and of event upon character or whether the action is arbitrary and contrived. In addition, the questions will consider film as film.

It may well be that in the past the movies have concentrated too heavily on the extraordinary and compelling surface reality of the medium instead of shaping an expression of the realities and passions of human existence as the poet does. But if, in addition to the comedies, westerns, and gangster pictures which are now inevitably part of our culture, movies like *On the Waterfront, A Raisin in the Sun, To Kill a Mockingbird, Lawrence of Arabia, David and Lisa, The Loneliness of the Long Distance Runner, Lord of the Flies,* and *Tom Jones* continue to be made, there is every chance that young people may grow to have a better understanding of the world in which they live and that the world may be a better place. For whether it is by a deliberate attempt or not, the function of all art is to enrich life by helping us to understand it, endure it, and value what is precious.

CHAPTER NINE

The Critical
Act

Good teachers of literature know literature intimately—the
good and the bad. They care so much about the first-rate works
of art that they do not despair because much writing—in pulp
magazines, slick magazines, or sex-horror-mystery paperbacks
—is unattractive, superficial, and sensational. They do not give
up because many of their students are naturally lured by literature of a sensational nature. They do not desert Shakespeare
and Shaw or Salinger and Malamud because of Mickey Spil-
lane or Little Orphan Annie.

As good teachers of film, they should know films intimately, the good and the bad, but principally the good. They
must care so much about John Huston's *The Red Badge of
Courage* and Jacques Tati's *Mr. Hulot's Holiday* that they do
not despair because many films appearing on the late, late show
are really dull, trite in plot, contrived, insincere. They must not
give up because many of their students have been reared on the
cheap triple-features of the drive-in theatres. They would not
desert Sergei Eisenstein and Jean Renoir or Robert Rossen
and Robert Flaherty because of the work of third-rate film
directors.

The teacher who discusses film in his classroom must know
films and film criticism. This book cannot show him the films;
he must take on that indispensable experience for himself. But
it indicates some of the range and depth of films and of film
criticism now available to him.

Consider reviews of the film *The Miracle Worker,* directed by Arthur Penn, produced by Fred Coe, and written by the author of the stage play, William Gibson. The reviews written by Bosley Crowther, Hollis Alpert, Brendan Gill, Stanley Kauffman, and Dwight Macdonald indicate the growing awareness of popular critics that film is a series of pictures rather than pages in a book or scenes in a play. Each of these critics comments on the visual communication of the film. Compare what critics say about the physical struggles which take place in the film between Annie Sullivan, the teacher, played by Anne Bancroft, and Helen Keller, the blind child, played by Patty Duke:

1

At one point, as they have their fierce physical battle (and battle of wills) in the Keller dining room, Penn has his camera not more than six inches from their distorted faces, without ever interrupting the movement of the long scene. This, alone, is a technical accomplishment, but it also makes for a marvelous vividness.[1]

Hollis Alpert

2

But because the physical encounters between the two in their strongly graphic roles of trained nurse and deaf-and-blind pupil seem to be more frequent and prolonged than they were in the play and are shown in close-ups, which dump the passion and violence right into your lap, the sheer rough-and-tumble of the drama becomes more dominant than it was on the stage.[2]

Bosley Crowther

[1] Hollis Alpert, in *Saturday Review,* May 26, 1962, p. 23.
[2] Bosley Crowther, in *The New York Times,* May 24, 1962, p. 29.

3

These encounters benefit in one way on the screen because the blind pantomime of Patty Duke is more effective when seen close. But Arthur Penn, director of the film as well as of the play, chose to make his camera "subjective" in these fights; it weaves, bobs, and whirls as the pair slam around the dining room and the cottage. This attempt to take us further "into" the scenes is, I think, mistaken. It makes us feel as if we were in these fights ourselves, which is an artily superficial effect, rather than letting us be moved by the effect of the fight on the two principals, which is the point of the scenes. It is like watching a prize-fight by ducking and circling with the boxers; we don't want to feel like one of the fighters; we want the effect of the opposition of *two* of them. As frequently happens when theatre directors make films, Penn has not quite dared not to use all the resources of the camera lest he be thought unadaptable.[3]

Stanley Kauffman

4

The intensity with which these two fierce adversaries wage war and at last make peace is heightened by the fact that the battleground is Arcady—a white Victorian house set in a slumberous, summery lawn, with, in the distance, ample barns, woods, and fields. This contrast between the action and its setting is something that only a camera could have provided, and Mr. Penn makes exceedingly effective use of it in transforming, and not merely disguising, the play with which Mr. Gibson and he began.[4]

Brendan Gill

[3] Stanley Kauffman, "Exercises in Pathos and Politics," reprinted from *The New Republic,* June 4, 1962, pp. 28-29. © Harrison-Blaine, Inc.
[4] Brendan Gill, "The Current Cinema—Out of the Dark," in *The New Yorker,* June 2, 1962, p. 79.

Mr. Alpert thought the fight scenes powerful, Mr. Crowther and Mr. Kauffman thought them too powerful, and Mr. Gill saw their pictorial setting as ironic.

A number of the reviewers commented unfavorably on the acting of Victor Jory, who played Helen Keller's father, and most of them found Inga Swenson's portrayal of her mother inadequate or wrong; for example,

5

Mr. Penn has allowed Victor Jory, never a subtle actor, to shout his way through Captain Keller and has mistakenly cast a flaccid actress, Inga Swenson, in the flaccid role of Mrs. Keller.[5]

Stanley Kauffman

6

Whether this is the role as Gibson has written it, or whether Miss Swenson is trying to extract more emotional juice than the role allows, I can't say, but in the case of Victor Jory's Captain Keller, I'm inclined to think that it is two-dimensional characterization which makes the Captain a figure of sound and fury, and little depth.[6]

Hollis Alpert

7

. . . Victor Jory, who overacts the overwritten father, Inga Swenson, who plays a doting, inept mother . . .[7]

Brendan Gill

[5] Kauffman, in op. cit.
[6] Alpert, in op. cit.
[7] Gill, in op. cit.

Producer Fred Coe and Director Arthur Penn have had long and distinguished careers in television drama and experience in making a remarkable but unheralded film called *The Left-Handed Gun* (a psychological study of Billy the Kid, played by Paul Newman), so they came to the task of creating a film out of a play with knowledge in the film medium, not as Mr. Kauffman implies, as neophytes. What Mr. Penn did in his most striking use of film was to superimpose pictures depicting Annie Sullivan's memory of her own tortured youth over shots of Annie Sullivan at the Kellers'. This filmic device drew censure from two critics:

8

Even condensed, the flashbacks about Annie's childhood and dead brother are irrelevant.[8]

Stanley Kauffman

9

. . . Annie Sullivans' hallucinatory recollections of her workhouse youth prove a pretentious distraction.[9]

Brendan Gill

10

. . . some effectively stylized flashbacks to Annie Sullivan's life in the Tewksbury orphanage.[10]

Dwight Macdonald

These passages depicting Annie's memory of her youth were superbly photographed and daringly edited as momentary

[8] Kauffman, in op. cit.
[9] Gill, in op. cit.
[10] Dwight Macdonald, in *Esquire,* January, 1963, pp. 110, 112, 114. © 1962, by Esquire, Inc.

images rather than developed sequences. They were introduced sporadically, as memories occur to us. For example, Annie's adult face appeared on the screen and overlaid on that, another shot of persons in her past, blurred in focus or whitened by overexposure to a snowy haziness not unlike that of pictures poorly received on a television screen. The figures of the past were ghostly, and their quick, half-heard comments carried an appropriately disturbing quality, but they asked too much of a viewer not intimately acquainted with the details of Annie's past life. They did not give added dimension to the story because their connections were not apparent to the viewer; often they were completely incoherent. They communicated the feeling of tortured memories; they failed to communicate the content of those memories. Perhaps that was all Arthur Penn intended, but if so, he was asking too much of the audience trained in watching commercial American films. Yet he may have intended just this, for in modern films being made in the United States as well as Europe and Japan and India, the most thoughtful and original directors, like our best modern poets and novelists, are asking more and more of their audiences. Dwight Macdonald says:

11

Making the audience work has never been popular in Hollywood, whose directors are trained to make everything clear, nudging us to the proper response. That "mood music" forever moaning and throbbing in the background, for example; a blind man could follow a film by Kazan or Kramer or Wyler. Antonioni's sound tracks on the contrary, are miracles of understatement, mostly using natural sounds, including the human voice, and often reversing the Hollywood pattern and stepping the sound *down,* or even eliminating it completely, during the "big scenes." He doesn't nudge, he states. The odd thing is that some of us in the movie audience, an increasing number of late years, rather enjoy doing some work, perhaps because we are used to books and paintings that require some effort from the consumer. This is incomprehensible to the successful Hollywood director—I've talked with a few—who invariably attribute my preference for Resnais, Kurosawa, Godard, Visconti, Bergman, Antonioni, *et al.,* to a combination of perversity and snobbishness. He cannot understand why one wants to pay for bread when one can get stones for nothing.[11]

The importance of films today is attested in various forms. A Gallup poll indicated that of adult Americans 50 percent (representing fifty-four million people) went to the movies, 46 percent (representing fifty million) read a book all the way through, 17 percent went to a basketball game or visited an art museum or attended a stage or theatrical production, 12 percent attended an adult education course.[12] Henry Popkin in "The Larger Audience" said that the film "is still the monarch of our mass media." [13] Although many trashy and ludicrous films are being created now, outnumbering the genuine works of art, the latter are growing as never before. The proliferation of film critics, film publications, film series (in and out of schools), and film festivals is further corroboration of the excellence and seriousness of the best contemporary films and their makers. A few years ago the student of film had only the critical works of classic film makers and critics to go to for education—books like Sergei Eisenstein's *Film Form* and *The Film Sense,* Rudolf Arnheim's *Film as Art,* V. I. Pudovkin's *Film Technique and Film Acting,* and Raymond Spottiswoode's *The Grammar of the Film.* But now in quarterlies like the British *Sight and Sound* and the American *Film Culture,*

---

[11] Macdonald, in *Esquire,* May, 1962. © 1962, by Esquire, Inc.
[12] *Council-Grams,* National Council of Teachers of English, XXIV: 2 (March, 1963).
[13] Robert E. Spiller (ed.), *A Time of Harvest* (New York, Hill and Wang, 1962), p. 124.

as well as *The Film Quarterly* and popular monthly magazines, he can find perceptive comment on films and film technique.

Here is an excerpt from a long review of Michelangelo Antonioni's method:

12

. . . I speak carefully when I say that I think he is making a new art form. . . . [He] is forging a new language apposite to a changed world. For a society theistically based and teleologically organized, the concepts of drama that derived substantially from Aristotle have sufficed for centuries. The film was born to that inheritance and, out of it, still produces fine works (although with a perceptibly increasing tinge of nostalgia). Antonioni has seen the dwindling force of this inheritance and is finding means to supplement it. He is achieving what many contemporary artists in his and other fields are seeking and not often with his success: renewal of his art rather than repetition.

. . . Antonioni, however, means to be making the miracle: finding a way to speak to us about ourselves today without crankily throwing away all that went before and without being bound by it. He is reshaping the idea of the content of film drama, discarding ancient and less ancient concepts, redirecting traditional audience expectation towards immersion in character rather than conflict of character. He is reshaping time itself in his films, taking it out of its customary synoptic form, wringing intensity out of its distention, daring to ask us to "live through" experiences with less distillation, deriving his drama from the very texture of such experiences and their juxtaposition, rather than from formal clash and climax and resolution. Fundamentally, he gives us characters whose drama consists in facing life minute after minute rather than in moving through organized plots with articulated obstacles; who have no well-marked cosmos to use as a tennis-player uses a court; who live and die without the implication of a divine eye that sees their virtues (whether men do or not) and cherishes them.[14]

Stanley Kauffman

Not only is such writing by critics now available to the student of film, but modern film makers are providing commentary which illuminates their original approach to the creative act.

13

"All art," said Robert Flaherty, "is a kind of exploring. To discover and reveal is the way every artist sets about his business." The explorers, the discoverers, are the transformers of the world. They are the scientist discovering in new fact new idea. Above all they are the artist, the poet, the seer, who out of the crucible of new fact and new idea bring new life, new power, new motive, and a deep refreshment. They discover for us the new image.

Robert Flaherty let the camera see everything, avid as a child, filled with childlike wonder. His pet word was "marvelous." Everything was marvelous, and his enthusiasm was equalled only by his patience. Patient as a scientist, he let the camera see everything exhaustively, and then, you remember, brought all this to the screen, and screened and screened it, and went out and shot again, for one reason only: to give the camera a chance to find that "moment of truth," that flash of perception, that penetration into the heart of the matter, which he knew the camera, left to itself, *could* find. The point in this process was that it was purely visual. Words played no part in it; it went beyond words. It was simply a degree of seeing. As ice turns to water and water to steam and a degree of temperature becomes a transformation, so a degree of seeing may become a transformation.

[14] Kauffman, "An Artist for an Age," reprinted from *The New Republic,* February 26, 1962, p. 27. © Harrison-Blaine, Inc.

. . . But above all he celebrates a new and strange and perhaps portentous fact, in the history of art a "first"—that the liberation of the spirit that comes from the profound experience of any great art can now come to us in a mass medium for a machine age through the medium of a machine. "On the spiritual plane, cinema is an invention every whit as important as on the material plane, the freeing of nuclear energy." [15]

These discussions, pointing up by contrast how thin is criticism by critics who are not themselves film makers, bring to the student the kind of insight available in books by Eisenstein, Kracauer, and Reisz, for example, but here applied to current approaches in film making. Flaherty, for instance, let his camera roam widely but then exercised considerable selection to whip so much footage into a work of art. Yet in the present surge of study and criticism of film, it is possible to obscure the fact that a few critics have always seen films for their visual qualities and written of them with insight and skill. Here, for example, is an excerpt from a review of John Ford's *The Grapes of Wrath* (a film discussed at length elsewhere in this book) written in 1940 by Otis Ferguson, a young critic of books, films, and jazz, who died in the second World War.

The film opens on a shot that strikes the whole mood of the piece like a chord: a half light, deep, empty space, a road stretching out of sight and a tall young man walking down it, with no other sound but his toneless approaching whistle. Then the truck, another road, the lank preacher, the deserted home and the dust blowing in the wind. Then by candlelight and with faces barely seen, the story of what happened, partly told and partly in flashbacks: the broken countryside. Then outside again, with the dust settling, and suddenly on the edge

[15] Frances Hubbard Flaherty, *The Odyssey of a Film-Maker; Robert Flaherty's Story* (Urbana, Ill., Beta Phi Mu, 1960), pp. 10-11, 40, 43. Last sentence quoted from Jean Debrix, "Cinema and Poetry," in *The Art of the Cinema.* Yale French Studies, No. 17 (New Haven: Payne and Lane, Summer 1956), p. 101.

of the horizon, the lights of a car: the law. Then morning; another road and mean house, and the Joad family at breakfast. It all moves with the simplicity and perfection of a wheel across silk.

When the truck rattles out onto the highway, leaving the open door and the dust blowing forlornly in the wind, there starts a series of great sweeping outdoor shots as beautifully tuned to purpose as anything you've seen . . . : clouds and space and the endless thrown ribbon of highway, with the truck going off and getting smaller, or coming down into the camera with growing roar and clank, or wheeling around the bend in that illusion of flight of a camera slowly panning to pick up and follow motion. Camps at night, a scene framed in low branches or the darkness around a lamp, fields rolling out in the sun, great pinnacles of rock, and back to the truck itself, and the long road.

• • •

Alfred Newman scored the music, but there again it's a good part John Ford music—which is to say almost none of the swelling theme stuff, a snatch of song here and there at night, a wheezy little parlor organ sometimes for the mother-and-son theme, and for the rest of the sounds of life—particularly fine here because this life is a cough and sputter and boom of motors up and down the roads. And Ford is not afraid to let silence be eloquent as it should be, or to use it as a background for the poignant train whistle, a mile off at night, for the going-away sequence.[16]

Otis Ferguson

Such film criticism as that of Otis Ferguson and Dwight Macdonald and Stanley Kauffman requires more than one seeing of a film and a special kind of involvement that is hard to bring about in the darkened theatre. For the motion picture viewer partially dissolves his identity among the others, who then with him constitute one collective spectator. He leaves

[16] Otis Ferguson, in *The New Republic,* February 12, 1940, p. 212.

his own reality far behind and participates vicariously in the action on the screen. The moving pictures draw him so powerfully into their stream that he becomes insensible of the structuring that makes up the stream. This insensibility is far more than Coleridge's "willing suspension of disbelief";[17] for most viewers it is a complete surrender of the disbelief, an abandonment of critical distance from the moment the lights go down and the screen credits appear.

Criticizing film is unusually demanding, but the finest creations of this medium, now only seventy years old, those which are works of art, deserve a disciplined response.

> . . . No other art can so powerfully exploit the dimensions of time and space. No other art has so many ways of involving a human being. It involves his eyes, ears, mind, heart, appetites all at once. It is drama, music, poetry, novel, painting at the same time. It is the whole of art in one art, and it demands the whole of man in every man. It seizes him and spirits him away into a dark cave; it envelops him in silence, in night. His inner eye begins to see, his secret ear begins to hear. Suddenly a vast mouth in the darkness opens and begins to utter visions. People. Cities. Rivers. Mountains. A whole world pours out of the mouth of the enraptured medium, and this world becomes the world of the man in the darkness watching.[18]

The extraordinary immediacy of the moving picture accounts not only for the difficulty in criticizing it but also for the willingness of the collective spectator to accept films that may be mediocre, whose characters are stock rather than unique, whose concepts are shabby, whose situations contrived, and whose values questionable. Motion pictures draw their viewers into them as a whirlpool draws objects into its vortex. Small wonder that on the one hand organizations whose chief

---

[17] Samuel Taylor Coleridge, *Biographia Literaria* (New York, Macmillan, 1926), p. 101.

[18] "A Religion of Film," *Time*, September 20, 1963, p. 82. Courtesy *Time;* copyright Time Inc., 1963.

concern has been the moral content of movies have early brought their attention to these powerful instruments, and on the other that poor movies continue to be made. Small wonder, too, that movies furnish so much of the current offering on television.

Because film employs the language of vision, the English teacher must bring new knowledge to his own viewing of it and to his teaching about it. This book has attempted to show how in helping students to see film more perceptibly, the teacher must do more than simply draw upon his knowledge of the strategies of literary art and human values—with which he is already familiar—and seek aid from viewing films and from the best critics of the medium. He must learn to watch films as *moving pictures,* seeing how a director and his fellow-workers select from the innumerable visual possibilities a detail (perhaps universal in its implications), a vast scene, a close-up, or a long shot; how they choose actors for their physical presence and direct them cinematically rather than theatrically, and how they exploit the devices of camera, lighting, sound, and scene for artistic purpose. Once the student begins to see film as film he may contribute even more than the teacher to such enlarging of perception in the classroom, for he himself is a child of the visual revolution.

A person studying film today may well feel that his perceptions of the medium are of more immediate import than those of a person studying literature, for film is still in its infancy. Popular critics can help those just beginning to see film as a visual medium that demands a newly aware and knowledgeable eye. To assess any art form in its pioneer stages is to feel a quickening of the pulse and surprising new awareness. That is the prospect which lies before the teacher and the student who come to the study and enjoyment of film genuinely open to new experience.

APPENDIX A

Teaching the Film

In some secondary schools, such as Washburn High School in Minneapolis and Bethesda-Chevy Chase High School, Montgomery County, Maryland, the administration preempts time from the daily schedule in which to show a complete film to the entire school. The students then return to their own classrooms and discuss the film from various standpoints and concerns, including technical features, photography, and music, as well as the setting, theme, and significance. . . . Such discussions are valuable to the extent that they discuss *film* as *film* and not as sociology or as items in a cross-media comparison. In many classes they furnish material for composition assignments.

In other systems, such as senior high schools in New Rochelle, New York, and Berkeley, California, films have been utilized in classes of slow students and of students not in college preparatory classes, with their primary aim a therapeutic one —to motivate slow learners, to engage hostile ones, or to spur the reading of books. While these ends are valuable in themselves and illustrative of the immense power of film to engage, such uses of film are not designed immediately to teach the study of film as art.

An experimental class in Denby High School, Detroit, has a number of suggested activities for evaluating films, among which is a project for making films within the school curriculum. Such a project can not help acquainting students directly with the principles of film making. Where time, space, and money are available, an activity involving the making of pic-

140

tures by students should result immediately in a heightened understanding of film technique and hence in more sensitive viewing.

Some schools, such as Broome Junior High School, Montgomery County, Maryland, combine the library with the audio-visual department in order to furnish the students with the resources of both and to provide viewing booths, with earphones, where one or more students may view film in the same manner in which he fulfilled a library assignment—outside of class time and outside of the classroom.

Norman Fruchter, a young American who has published a novel, taught six film courses in two years' work in the English and Social Studies Department at Kingsway Day College in London. A detailed account of his experience appeared as "two 2 hours a week" in *Sight and Sound,* Autumn, 1962. The following passage from the article indicates his point of view and approach.

I started the First Film Course by accident. During a wave of unofficial strikes soon after the High Court judgment in the ETU case, I was talking about trade unions with a class of police cadets doing English and Social Studies. I asked if anyone had seen *The Angry Silence.*

"Who was in it?" I named some of the actors. The cadet shook his head. "Nah. Couldn't have been a good film. Didn't have no stars."

I asked what made a good film. Most of the cadets said that stars made the film; a few thought the story was more important. But they all talked about a film as something that just happened, right across the Gaumont screen. They had no realisation that a film takes shape from the conscious choice of producer and director, who make it, and sell it, as a product. They could name no directors, and no one recognized the half-dozen names I threw out. They saw films as facts, events, which they either liked or didn't.

The class ended, and I thought about what they'd said,

and tried to remember how I'd watched films at seventeen or eighteen. I think I watched films much as they described—involved, or not involved, responding, or not responding. I never thought about the people who made a film, or how it was made, or even how it differed from last week's film. I wondered how I would have reacted if anyone had asked me to study films instead of just go to them; and decided to try a film course during the last four weeks of term.

I made what I hope is the maximum number of mistakes. I thought I had to begin by teaching, formally, terms like long-shot, close-up, dissolve, wipe, cut and pan, which I felt the class had to understand and be able to use before we could talk about films properly. Through Paddy Whannel, Education Officer at the British Film Institute, I got a fine series of film extracts and advice about how to begin that would have saved me a good many hours, had I listened. But I showed far too much film, left far too little time for discussion. I showed *The Great Train Robbery* the first week, with extracts from Clouzot's *Wages of Fear* and Reed's *The Third Man,* and the whole of Reisz and Richardson's *Momma Don't Allow*—fifty-eight minutes of screen time out of ninety class minutes. The second week I did even better: sixty-two minutes of film. The few points I could make were scattered and hurried; little chance for discussion occurred and almost no opportunity to learn anything. The third week I tried a feature, *Paths of Glory;* the cadets liked it, though many of them disagreed with its direction. More important, they began to talk in terms of what they had seen on the screen, rather than registering initial responses. I found that instead of asking "Did you like it?" I could ask, "How does this scene work?" . . .[1]

---

[1] Norman Fruchter, "two 2 hours a week," *Sight and Sound,* Autumn, 1962. Reprinted here by permission of *Sight and Sound.*

Film as Sharpener
of Perception

WILLIAM D. BAKER

While we nibble away at other rhetorical precepts—be specific, avoid generalities, focus on a single aspect of the subject, narrow the topic—our primary need is for something to help students learn to look at and record the details that make meaning.

My purpose is to explain a seldom used technique for teaching students to look at details: film analysis. This technique engages students in the act of discovering what life and language have to offer. Students enjoy film and can be taught to analyze it; hence it makes sense to use this means to plunge them into the act of discovery.

Film enters the realm of art in its form and its use of symbols. We may start with the assumption that the poet and the film director are both deliberate artists. That is, they don't let a word or a scene just "happen-in" by itself. John Ciardi, poetry editor of the *Saturday Review,* says that "To speak of things 'happening-in' is to assault the integrity of a poem. Poetry cannot be discussed meaningfully unless one can assume that everything in the poem—every last comma and variant spelling—is in it by the poet's specific act of choice. Only bad poets allow into their poems what is haphazard or cheaply chosen." Assuming that the best film directors are poets, we

Dr. Baker is Dean of the Faculty at Rockford College, Rockford, Illinois. This article first appeared in the February 1964 issue of *College Composition and Communication* and is reprinted with the permission of the author.

can ask "Why that scene there? Why that dissolve? Why that music? Why does the actor walk from right to left? Why that long shot? Why that close-up? Why that camera angle?" And on and on. We should assume that nothing "happens-in."

For a partial list of kinds of choices one may ask of the director, see Rudolph Arnheim's catalog of montage effects in *Film as Art* (University of California Press, 1957, pp. 94-98). Because it is readily available in paperback, Arnheim's book is a good place to start. The point is to begin with the technique, not the message, of the film. No student, from kindergarten to college, enters the study of film with a clean, blank slate of nonexperience. Would that he would. He has seen film, has been brought up on it, and resists an analysis of it because he has trained himself to concentrate on the message. Hence, he must learn to disregard the message temporarily, just as a good stenographer disregards the message when she transcribes her shorthand. Afterwards, she checks for sense and message. So start with something like Arnheim. Work up a vocabulary of film analysis. Then begin to analyze a short film as carefully and thoughtfully as you would a poem.

I suggest a short film like *The River* (directed by Pare Lorentz, produced by the United States Department of Agriculture, 1909). Note how it heightens an effect here, bridges a gap there and transmits in its total effect the sense of river to land to people. Note the absence of people until the film is well underway. Note . . . well, the cataloging could go on, but you must do it for yourself. Your sensitivity will tell you what to note, and if you have disciplined yourself to think ahead of the story, as a conductor thinks ahead of the orchestra, you will find yourself considering alternatives to the film director's choice. And to consider an artist's alternatives is to judge his art.

As an initial assignment after the showing of the film, I have tried with success asking the students to make up a short dramatic plot and then write it as they would film it, with shooting directions in the margin. Afterwards they criticized each other's scripts and challenged the why of a close-up here and the wherefore of a long shot there.

Experience shows that students do not immediately see the relationship between film analysis and rhetorical principles. You must teach them the relationship, as carefully as some teachers (fie on them) teach sentence diagramming, slowly, thoroughly, item by item.

Item: A close-up is sometimes a detail. This is an example on film. See it? This is an example in writing. See it? Now find an example of each on your own.

Item: A long shot is sometimes a generalization. This is an example on film. See it? Translate it into a written generalization. Now find a generalization in a current novel or poem and translate it into a long shot on film. Describe the position of the camera, how it moves, what it sees.

Item: The announcer says, "The crowd went wild with joy." How would a film show this? Use both close-ups and long shots.

Item: A student writes, "I used to be afraid to attend any kind of social gathering, but now I enjoy parties because I have more confidence in myself." Write the script of a short film indicating how the camera would convey the above message. Use a flashback in your script. When you have finished, comment on the difference between the student's writing and the camera's message.

Item: Now translate the film script into a theme, keeping it as visual as possible.

Item: For honors students: show how Alfred Hitchcock's depiction of a scene differs from that of John Huston.

Item: Find a short poem and indicate how you would convey its message on film. Once students are engaged in a debate about film it is difficult for them to look at a television play with the same old eyes, and for those who get carried away (perhaps mirroring the teacher's enthusiasm) they will not be able to get on a bus, or walk across the campus, or go to a football game with the same old eyes. They will begin to see things in close-ups and long shots. They will begin to focus on the significant details and maneuver the camera angle until they tell the story. They will begin to see that only by dividing "hot" from a thermometer reading may one speak of a "sense of heat." They will begin to see that neither a collection of long shots nor a jumble of close-ups by themselves can convey the message. There needs to be an assembly according to pre-determined principles. What is the sense to be conveyed? Now we are back to the principles of rhetoric. Unity, coherence, emphasis. Shun the generalization, use the detail, limit the topic, focus on a significant aspect. The words have been in rhetoric texts for centuries, and film analysis is but a new twist to the old tried-and-true principles.

APPENDIX C

References

BOOKS

Agee, James. *Agee on Film* and *Five Film Scripts*. [New York: Mc-Dowell, Obolensky, Inc., 1958-1960.] 2 volumes.

Volume I contains articles by Agee. As a critic for *The Nation* and *Time,* his observations were perceptive, candid, and entertaining. *Agee on Film* makes acute observations on films, directors, and writers, as well as assessing the content of the films discussed. Agee was aware of film as art—not merely passive entertainment. The first volume also contains a brilliant chapter on "Comedy's Greatest Era" and a fine article on director John Huston.

Volume II contains five of his scripts, including his script for *The African Queen.*

Alpert, Hollis. *The Dreams and the Dreamers.* New York: Macmillan, 1962. 258 pp.

Staff writer for the *Saturday Review,* the author reveals an increasing knowledge of cinematic technique, in this collection of informal essays which includes the especially perceptive "Film and Theater."

Arnheim, Rudolf. *Film as Art.* Berkeley and Los Angeles: University of California Press, 1957. 250 pp. Paper.

Arnheim's classic book on film aesthetics shows how film goes beyond photography into the realm of art. He examines fundamental film principles, including a study of the time-space continuum, techniques for capturing or suggesting point of view, and the artistry of juxtaposition. An enthusiast of the silent films, Arnheim chooses his most vivid illustrations from early silent motion pictures. He effectively compares techniques used in film and theatre.

Bergman, Ingmar. *Four Screenplays of Ingmar Bergman.* New York: Simon and Schuster, 1960. 330 pp.

In an introduction Bergman discusses film making. The scripts include those for *The Seventh Seal* and *Wild Strawberries*.

Bluestone, George. *Novels into Film*. Baltimore: Johns Hopkins, 1957. Also Berkeley: University of California Press, 1961. Paper.

In a detailed study of film as a visual, verbal, and aural medium, Bluestone contrasts the novel and film as media; he notes fundamental similarities and essential differences. The problem of translation from novel to film is examined in superb detail, using six films for specific study. These include *The Informer, Wuthering Heights, Pride and Prejudice, The Grapes of Wrath, The Ox-Bow Incident,* and *Madame Bovary*.

Boutwell, William D. *Using Mass Media in the Schools*. New York: Appleton-Century-Crofts, 1962. 292 pp. Also available from National Council of Teachers of English.

An excellent preface by Mr. Boutwell is followed by a discussion of the anatomy of mass media, including motion pictures. There are sections on what teachers can do and are doing with all forms of mass media of communication.

Crowther, Bosley. *Movies and Censorship*. Public Affairs Pamphlet, No. 332 (New York: Public Affairs Committee, 1962). 28 pp. $.25.

This brief historical discussion of censorship of films and moderate, reasonable judgments is easy to follow, not searching or profound.

Eisenstein, Sergei M. *Film Form and the Film Sense*. [New York: Harcourt, Brace & World, 1949.] Cleveland: World, Meridian MGIO.

Eisenstein, one of the all-time great film directors and film theorists, discusses his film philosophy. He emphasizes the structure of film, rejecting trick photography. In *Film Form,* he notes the relationship of Japanese hokku poetry to basic film principles. He describes montage, an important film structure, as conflict and relates it to counterpoint techniques. The book contains a particularly fine chapter on "The Structure of the Film."

Film and Television in Education for Teaching. A report of a Joint Working Party of the Association of Teachers in Colleges and Departments of Education and the British Film Institute. London: British Film Institute, no date [after 1959]. 66 pp. Two shillings. (81 Dean Street, London, W. 1, England)

Directed to groups in the film industry, television producers, educational administrators, and those preparing teachers, the account emphasizes the deep influence of film and television. Both deserve study. Methods and possible courses are indicated.

Fischer, Edward. *The Screen Arts*. New York: Sheed and Ward, 1960. 184 pp.

This is an uncomplicated presentation written in familiar style.

Fulton, A. R. *Motion Pictures: The Development of an Art from Silent Films to the Age of Television*. Norman, Oklahoma: University of Oklahoma Press, 1960.

This excellent historical background on films includes a detailed study of editing by early directors like David W. Griffith. Fulton has devoted a valuable chapter to the technique of montage. He also contrasts media in three film chapters: "From Play to Film," "From Novel to Film," and "From Short Story to Film." The book contains a very useful chapter on television. Concrete illustrations supplement the astute observations.

Gassner, John, and Nichols, Dudley. *Twenty Best Film Plays*. New York: Crown, 1943. 1112 pp.

Among the scripts for twenty film plays are those for *Rebecca, Wuthering Heights, The Grapes of Wrath, How Green Was My Valley, The Life of Emile Zola, Juarez, The Good Earth, All That Money Can Buy* ("The Devil and Daniel Webster"), *Yellow Jack,* and *The Fight for Life.*

Jacobs, Lewis. *The Rise of the American Film*. New York: Harcourt, Brace & World, 1939. O.P.

Jacobs recaptures the excitement of film history by an examination of many of the films that made motion picture history. He ranges from Méliès to Disney, and includes a fine chapter on D. W. Griffith, a stimulating chapter on "A Throng of Directors," as well as valuable information in the section on "Refinements in Technique." Jacobs appends a good bibliography; copious details make this a first-rate reference work.

Jacobs, Lewis. *Introduction to the Art of the Movies*. New York: Noonday N149, 1960.

This bright collection of essays on film is conveniently short.
Knight, Arthur. *The Liveliest Art*. New York: Macmillan, 1957.

A panoramic, eminently readable survey of the growth of the industry, technical innovations, the star system, and international trends is well indexed. A fine ready reference book.

Kracauer, Siegfried. *Theory of Film*. New York: Oxford, 1960.

Kracauer assumes film to be an extension of photography; he places his emphasis on a study of the visual elements of film. He examines the major film propensities and techniques for achieving aesthetic effects. The section of the book describing the "found story" and the episode as raw material for film is excellent. Kracauer's comparison of the novel and film media is extremely well done. The book also examines the use of innovations in the history of film making.

Lindgren, Ernest. *The Art of the Film, an Introduction to Film*. New York: Macmillan, 1948.

This is an excellent and discerning primer of technique and theory. It is illustrated.

MacCann, Richard Dyer. *Hollywood in Transition*. Boston: Houghton Mifflin, 1962. 208 pp.

This lucid and carefully documented survey of the movie industry in its present crisis, challenged both by foreign films and television, was written by a man who has been both reporter (*Christian Science Monitor*) and teacher (the University of Southern California). It is especially useful for its analysis of the reasons for Hollywood's present state.

Mallery, David. *The School and the Art of Motion Pictures*. A Challenge to Teachers. Boston: National Association of Independent Schools, 1964. 101 pp. (4 Liberty Square, Boston, Massachusetts)

Part One tells of the new enthusiasm for film and its respectability, giving implications for concern for film in schools. Part Two divides films by topics—biography, comedy, western, for example—and tells of outstanding films now available for rental to schools in 16mm. Many of the film comments are Mr. Mallery's own, based on his experience, revealing what might be helpful to schools.

Nicoll, Allardyce. *Film and Theatre*. New York: Crowell, 1936.

Nicoll, a famous scholar whose primary interest is the theatre, compares film and theatre as art media; he also outlines a set of basic film principles related to artistic expression. Nicoll concludes that film and theatre will go independent paths. Noting existing theatrical traditions, he forecasts original film traditions. Very acutely, he argues for a cinema repertory. Other interesting sections of this book examine problems in filming Shakespearian drama and stress the desirability of "emotional acceptance" plus "intellectual analysis" of film.

Peters, J. L. M. *Teaching About the Film.* New York: International Documents Service (a division of the Columbia University Press), 1961. 120 pp. (2960 Broadway, New York, New York)

Commissioned by UNESCO, this slender book shows concern for protecting young people particularly from the faults and excesses of mass media by awakening and developing a critical spirit—a spirit of discrimination or appreciation. The teaching of film appreciation is attracting attention in many parts of the world. A kind of handbook on teaching about film, the book is based largely on the ideas of those in a number of countries. The author, convinced that film and television are becoming a kind of "second world" for young people, believes it is urgent for education to take note of the new environment in which youth lives visually. The book contains excellent illustrations and a bibliography.

Pudovkin, V. I. *Film Technique and Film Acting.* New York: Lear Publishers, 1949. 357 pp. Also in paper: New York: Grove, Evergreen E248, 1960. 388 pp.

In their directness the titles of these two books suggest their content: detailed, clear discussion of how a director should make a film. Classic works, first published abroad in 1929 and 1933, Pudovkin's two books (published now in one volume) never lose themselves in critical terms or theory, but with many examples illuminate the process of film much as Stanislavsky's *An Actor Prepares* illuminates the process of drama.

Ramsaye, Terry. *A Million and One Nights.* A History of the Motion Picture. New York: Simon and Schuster, 1964. Paper.

First printed in the 1920's and recently reissued.

Reisz, Karel. *The Technique of Film Editing*. New York: Focal, 1961. 288 pp. (Distributed in New York by AMPhoto, 33 West 60 Street, New York, New York)

Karel Reisz, director and writer, had the guidance of a committee appointed by the British Film Academy. Therold Dickinson, chairman, was assisted by nine members, including David Lean and Ernest Lindgren. Some critics place the book first among interpretations of film. Concerned chiefly with the manipulation of photography and the process of editing, it is a distinct help in understanding subtleties in the use of visual images to achieve the end sought by a director. To indicate ways of editing, it refers to specific films and sequences. Film editing involves many aspects of film production; the relationship is indicated.

Rosenberg, Bernard, and White, David (Eds.) *Mass Culture: the Popular Arts in America*. New York: Free Press, 1957.

Here is a noteworthy collection of essays examining literature, comic strips, television, radio, advertising, and of course the movies, all in the social context of American popular culture.

Ross, Lillian. *Picture*. New York: Rinehart, 1952. 258 pp. Garden City, N.Y.: Doubleday, Dolphin C390.

The entire book is devoted to a study of the making of the movie, *The Red Badge of Courage,* almost without comment by Miss Ross. It succeeds in showing the terrible odds that confront the able and inspired director (in this case John Huston) as his picture is relentlessly cheapened by authority.

Rotha, Paul, and Griffith, Richard. *The Film Till Now*. London: Vision Press and Mayflower Publishing Company, 1949. New York: Funk and Wagnalls, 1949.

In this 800-page volume, Rotha surveys the historical world of film including American, British, French, Russian, and German films. In another section, Asian and Latin American film developments are assessed. Over 175 still shots illustrate significant American and foreign films from 1898 through 1948. The Griffith section brings the book up to date. Useful chapters are devoted to documentary films and cartoons. There is also an illuminating chapter on directors, writers, and producers.

Schmidt, Georg, Schmalenbach, Werner, and Bächlin, Peter. *The Film: Its Economic, Social, and Artistic Problems.* London: Falcon, 1948. Illustrated.

The Swiss authors present the fiction film as influential and as revealing cultural problems. "In the film all visible things act."

Spottiswoode, Raymond. *A Grammar of the Film.* Berkeley: University of California Press, 1950.

The subtitle, "An Analysis of Film Technique," suggests the emphasis. Recognizing the unique power of film as an art form, Spottiswoode suggests that "discontinuities" contribute to cinematic force. Camera speeds, film techniques, and static vs. dynamic film making are studied in detail. He deplores commercial domination tending toward stereotyping for profit and attacks the inclination of many film makers to be imitative.

Talbot, Daniel. *Film: An Anthology.* New York: Simon and Schuster, 1959.

This superb collection of articles on film includes pieces by James Agee, Rudolf Arnheim, Sergei Eisenstein, Jean Cocteau, Rene Clair, Lewis Jacobs, and Susanne Langer—among many others. Articles cover analysis of films, film genres, and the social content of pictures. A major section of the book is devoted to the theory and technique of film making. The concluding section deals with historical and personal recollections by perceptive writers on film personalities.

Tyler, Parker. *Classics of the Foreign Film.* New York: Citadel, 1962.

This pictorial treasury combines excellent photographs and stills and an extremely well-written text. It introduces significant directors ranging from Eisenstein to Antonioni. Seventy-five film classics are described and discussed, beginning with *The Cabinet of Dr. Caligari* (1919) and concluding with *La Notte* (1961). The short discussions are lucid and valuable, well-written and incisive. A minor quibble would be the omission of Truffaut's *The Four Hundred Blows* (1960).

Warshow, Robert. *The Immediate Experience.* Garden City, N.Y.: Doubleday, 1962. 282 pp.

This book examines American popular culture and American films, with additional chapters concentrating on Chaplin and the art film. Warshow understands the nature of the film impact on audiences; he is not limited to aesthetics or an attack on film as popular culture. He has particularly fine chapters on "The Gangster as Tragic Hero" and "The Westerner." His detailed study of the success of Hollywood's tribute to America in *The Best Years of Our Lives* is extremely informative.

Williams, Raymond, and Orrom, Michael. *Preface to Film*. London: Film Drama Limited, 1954. 129 pages.

The authors show the relation of film to dramatic tradition and look into the future of film entertainment.

Wolfenstein, Martha, and Leites, Nathan. *Movies: A Psychological Study*. New York: Free Press, 1950.

The authors begin with day dreams, universal day dreams, and examine how day dreams are turned to film purposes. They study American films for recurrent themes; then they examine the treatment accorded those themes by American, British, and French films. Their insights are sharp and revealing. The insights revealed, for example, by their "good-bad girl" analysis of American films are brilliant; so is the rest of the chapter on "Lovers and Loved Ones." This is a perceptive analysis of film content.

PERIODICALS

American Cinematographer; the Magazine of Motion Picture Photography. (American Society of Cinematographers) ASC Agency, Inc., 1782 North Orange Drive, Hollywood 28, California. $4.

Film Culture. CPO Box 1499, New York 1, New York. $3.

This quarterly, a solid yet provocative journal spear-headed by Jonas Mekas, ranges from notes on experimental film shorts to articles by Europe's most distinguished directors.

Film Daily Yearbook of Motion Pictures. The Film Daily, 1501 Broadway, New York 36, New York.

This annual publication is a most valuable source of information about motion pictures.

Filmfacts. P.O. Box 53, Village Station, 150 Christopher Street, New York, New York. $20 a year.

Illustrated. This weekly presents synopses and critiques of features.

Films in Review. National Board of Review of Motion Pictures, Inc., 31 Union Square, New York 3, New York. Monthly October through May; bimonthly June-July, August-September. $5.

Film Quarterly. Berkeley, California, University of California Press. $4.

Sight and Sound; the International Film Quarterly. [British Film Institute, 81 Dean Street, London, W. 1, England.] Eastern News Distributors, Inc., 255 Seventh Avenue, New York 1, New York. $3.50.

This British film quarterly gives searching criticism of films from all over the world and also exceptional still shots reproduced from films.

ARTICLES ON FILMS

"The Anti-Formula Film," *Saturday Review,* December 28, 1963, pp. 13-24.

Six articles on the new cinema—men, ideas, and problems —are by Hollis Alpert, Richard Boeth, James Fixx, Arthur Knight, Ralph Schoenstein, and Lyn Tornabene.

Alden, Alex E. "Engineering Standards for Theater and Television Motion Pictures," *The Magazine of Standards,* May 7, 1963. American Standards Association, 10 East 40 Street, New York 16, New York.

Motion pictures benefit from the emphasis on engineering standardization.

Barr, Charles. "CinemaScope: Before and After," *Film Quarterly,* Summer, 1963, pp. 4-24.

This article contains reviews of many books about film.

Culkin, Rev. John M., S.J. "A High School Film Festival," *The Catholic Educator,* February, 1964, pp. 596-599.

Twenty-four high school juniors and seniors attended a three-week festival of six films. The festival was planned because of the importance of film study and a desire to test the validity of the "see and discuss" method.

Culkin, Rev. John M., S.J. "Mass Media Study in the Schools,"

National Catholic Educational Association Bulletin, February, 1963, pp. 12-28.

Based on a talk given at a convention of the National Council of Teachers of English, the article is specific about the need for study of the mass media and methods of doing so.

Limbacher, James L. "Widescreen Chronology: Widescreen Experimentation Is Almost as Old as the Movies Themselves," *Journal of the Society of Motion Picture and Television Engineers,* February, 1956. (Reprinted from *Films in Review,* October, 1955.)

The author presents a compact account of experimenters, their processes, and titles of films in which the processes were used.

Mayer, Arthur. "How Much Can the Movies Say?" *Saturday Review,* November 3, 1962, pp. 18-20, 52-53.

"The Movies," Special Double Issue, *Life,* December 20, 1963, pp. 4-188.

Thirteen articles present movies as an international language of increasingly greater depth.

Ong, Rev. Walter J., S.J. "Wired for Sound: Teaching, Communications, and Technological Culture," *College English,* February, 1960, pp. 245-251.

The new media are not gadgets but part of a shift affecting ideas of communication, a basis for speculation on type (typography) in relation to sight and sound.

Wide-Screen Motion Pictures. Society of Motion Picture and Television Engineers, 9 East 41 Street, New York 17, New York. 18 pp. (being revised).

This publication gives brief, authoritative information.

16 mm. Film Sources

American Art and History Films, 41 W. 47th Street, New York 36, New York

American Museum of Natural History Film Library, 77th Street and Central Park W., New York, New York

Association Films, Broad at Elm, Ridgefield, New Jersey

Athena Films, 165 W. 46th Street, New York 36, New York

Brandon Films, 200 W. 57th Street, New York City 19, New York

British Information Services, 13 E. 37th Street, New York 16, New York

Center for Mass Communication, Columbia University, 1125 Amsterdam Avenue, New York 25, New York

Churchill Films, 6671 Sunset Boulevard, Los Angeles 28, California

Cinema Guild, 10 Fiske Place, Mount Vernon, New York

Cinema 16, 175 Lexington Avenue, New York 16, New York

Contemporary Films, 13 E. 37th Street, New York City 16, New York

Coronet Films, 65 E. South Water Street, Chicago, Illinois

Disney Productions, 16 mm. Division, 2400 West Alameda Avenue, Burbank, California

Encyclopaedia Britannica Films, 1150 Wilmette Avenue, Wilmette, Illinois

Film Associates of California, 11014 Santa Monica Boulevard, Los Angeles 25, California

Film Images, 1860 Broadway, New York 23, New York

Films, Inc., 1150 Wilmette Avenue, Wilmette, Illinois

Franco-American Distribution Center, 972 Fifth Avenue, New York 22, New York

Ideal Pictures, 58 E. South Water Street, Chicago 1, Illinois

International Film Bureau, 332 S. Michigan Avenue, Chicago, Illinois

McGraw-Hill Text Films, 330 W. 42nd Street, New York 36, New York

Modern Talking Picture Service, 3 E. 54th Street, New York 22, New York

N.E.T. Film Service, Indiana University, Bloomington, Indiana

National Film Board of Canada, 680 Fifth Avenue, New York, New York

Pictura Films, 487 Park Avenue, New York 22, New York

Productions Unlimited, 1564 Broadway, New York, New York

Rembrandt Films, 59 E. 54th Street, New York 22, New York

Sutherland Films, 201 N. Occidental Boulevard, Los Angeles 26, California

Teaching Film Custodians, Inc., 25 W. 43rd Street, New York 36, New York

Trans-World Films, 53 W. Jackson Boulevard, Chicago 4, Illinois

United World Films, 1445 Park Avenue, New York 29, New York

Index of Films

159

General Index